"Great news, tipplers pinch-faced scolds, a. Knocking a couple back at the local bar is *good* for you. In *The Joy of Tippling*, sociologist and inveterate tippler Ray Oldenburg tells us why, backed up with solid research, indisputable facts and real news, all cheerfully served with dash and wit."

— John Tebeau, author of *Bars, Taverns, and Dives New Yorkers Love*

"Ray Oldenburg's charming, reasoned ode to tippling and taverns—to moderate social drinking and the places where this occurs—is just the book America needs now. I wish every politician would read it and take its lessons to heart."

— David Wondrich, author of *Imbibe!*

"Ray Oldenburg proves what wise tipplers already know: that drinking alcohol, in moderation and in warm company, is good for you. Reading *The Joy of Tippling* is like sitting on a barstool next to your smartest, most charming friend; it's an edifying experience you'll want to return to again and again."

— St. John Frizell, restaurateur, bartender, and *Men's Journal* drinks correspondent

A Salute to Bars, Taverns, and Pubs

by
**RAY OLDENBURG**
author of
*The Great Good Place*

**BERKSHIRE** PUBLISHING GROUP

Published by:
Berkshire Publishing Group LLC
Great Barrington, Massachusetts 01230
www.berkshirepublishing.com

Printed in the United States of America.

**Library of Congress Cataloging-in-Publication Data**
Names: Oldenburg, Ray, author.
Title: The joy of tippling : a salute to bars, taverns, and pubs (with recipes) / by Ray Oldenburg.
Description: Great Barrington, MA : Berkshire Publishing Group, [2019] | Includes index.
Identifiers: LCCN 2018011471 (print) | LCCN 2018020516 (ebook) | ISBN 9781614728375 (ebook) | ISBN 9781614728382 (pbk.)
Subjects: LCSH: Cocktails. | Alcoholic beverages—History. | Alcoholic beverages—Social aspects. | Drinking of alcoholic beverages—History. | Drinking of alcoholic beverages—Social aspects. | Entertaining.
Classification: LCC GT2884 (ebook) | LCC GT2884 .O55 2018 (print) | DDC
394.1/3—dc23
LC record available at https://lccn.loc.gov/2018011471

The cover photo of bartender David Guenette was taken at Number Ten, in Great Barrington, Massachusetts, where Berkshire Publishing is located. Photograph by Vijay Das, used with kind permission of proprietor Vern Kennedy.

# Contents

# *Foreword*

---

I first met Ray Oldenburg some four decades ago through colleagues who were impressed with the originality and brilliance of his work on community. We've been friends ever since. Ray's masterpiece, *The Great Good Place: Cafés, Coffee Shops, Community Centers, Beauty Parlors, General Stores, Bars, Hangouts, and How They Get You Through the Day*, was published in 1989. It has become the gold standard for work on the importance of community and how much voluntary associations in public places contribute to our lives, our health, our happiness, and our overall sense of well-being.

*The Joy of Tippling* is very much in the same tradition. Here he focuses on one particular aspect of good times: drinking or "tippling." The word tipple, Ray explains, may have evolved from the Norwegian word *tipla*, which means to drink slowly. A tippler is, there-fore, is someone who drinks habitually but moderately.

Even though, as Ray points out, saloons and tav-erns were among the first structures built in America as the country marched westward, some early settlers also brought with them a series of dour puritanical be-liefs that saw anything that smacked of good times as suspicious, if not downright evil.

Such an attitude, captured nicely in H. L. Menck-en's famous definition of Puritanism—"The haunting fear that someone, somewhere, may be happy"—persists to this day in a culture that officially values work over play, abstemiousness over letting go, and readiness over relaxation, at least when in public. At home, of course, it is a different matter. There the consumption of alco-holic beverages may occur without the opprobrium that attaches itself to public drinking, though as Ray points out there are regional differences, with tipplers from Southern states more likely to take their drinking plea-sures at home (perhaps out of fear that a fellow Baptist will see them going into a bar and make a fuss about it). Such a division reinforces the fear that drinking might lead to drunkenness, a sin that must be avoided at all costs lest our friends, neighbors, or colleagues see us as anything other than sober and restrained.

The trump card of the puritans is the slippery and much abused word *health*, a word that Oscar Wilde called "the silliest word in the English language." Label something "unhealthy" and the case is closed in the minds of many Americans. At the end of this convoluted logic is a diminution of the places of enjoyment in a well-rounded life. This book is primarily about happiness, celebration, and the role that alcohol plays in the good times we relish and share. Critics might retort that there is no way to go back to those idyllic times and places and we are destined to live the sterile lives offered by our current arrangements. Ray disagrees. Hear him out as he goes through studies from sociologists, anthropologists, epidemiologists, and historians, and you'll see that it doesn't have to be this way.

The concept of "third place," first developed in *The Great Good Place*, argued that Americans are increasingly dominated by a "two-stop" model of life. These two stops—home and work—"conjoined by the ordeal of commuting," left out the all-important community-based "third place." These places of pure sociability, such as bars and taverns, help keep people in touch with their common humanity, give vent to feelings that can't easily be expressed at home or work, and lend badly needed perspective to life. The "loosened tongue" that is usually attributed to the physiological effects of booze may be much more a function of the liberating environments of these third places than the effects of alcohol itself.

So, as Ray points out, one of the most salutary qualities of alcohol, contrary to puritan fears, is its contribution to the very foundation of community. All of his examples include face-to-face interaction and encourage walking instead of driving. He urges us to turn off the television and put away our "pocket gods."

By now a recognized expert on community, Ray followed up *The Great Good Place* with a companion volume entitled *Celebrating the Third Place*, which brought together a series of inspiring stories about the ways that particular third places transformed the spaces in which they were located. These stories are notable because they show it can still be done and without sacrificing the financial benefits that owners seek. These are but the preliminaries to the rollicking good read that is before you. While the work is in some sense about varieties of drinks and drinking, the larger theme is about fellowship, laughter, the company of others, and the joys of life. Here you'll learn bar and tavern dos and don'ts, and find pith and wisdom from the likes of Fran Lebowitz ("Never allow children to mix drinks. It is unseemly and they use too much vermouth") and Pappy Maverick ("Never cry over spilt milk. It could have been whiskey").

Did you know, for example, that the Greek poet Anacreon was noted for his drinking songs and that "To Anacreon in Heaven" was a favorite drinking song of the Anacreon Society in London? You should, because Francis Scott Key set the words of our national anthem to it. Or that beer was the first alcoholic beverage imported by the colonists, but it was soon overtaken by rum? Or that the first spirits were distilled in Staten Island in 1640? Or that only women work on the bottling line at Russia's famous Stolichnaya vodka factory to keep men from temptation? I didn't think so.

The last half of the book is a treasure filled with ephemeral knowledge about virtually every category of booze. With encyclopedia-like attention to detail, Oldenburg celebrates the tastes, history, folklore, and culture of beer, wine, and distilled spirits of all kinds. He analyzes the Talmudic disputes about the Martini's proper ratio of gin to vermouth and concludes that it is half and half. He also notes that the Manhattan is making a comeback.

I can't resist pointing out that without alcohol we might never have had the brilliant writing of the late journalist Hunter S. Thompson. "I would sit down at a long table with a typewriter and two bottles of Wild Turkey and proceed until the article was done and the bottles were empty." The same is true for countless Nobel Prize winners in literature. God only knows what literary masterpieces were composed under the influence of alcohol. Be that as it may, this is *not* what Oldenburg means by the term *tippling*.

For those readers who still appreciate a good laugh to go with their intellectual stimulation, this book is for you and all we can do is offer a toast:

MAZELTOV!

Charles EDGLEY
University of Arkansas at Little Rock

# 1

# *A Search for Community*

My first plea for the return of some semblance of community in the United States was published late in 1989.
The book was entitled *The Great Good Place: Cafés, Coffee Shops, Community Centers, Beauty Parlors, General
Stores, Bars, Hangouts, and How They Get You Through
the Day,* and the core idea was that we all need a place
apart from home and work where we can relax in warm
company and be ourselves, outside the roles we play in
the family and on the job. In such places we meet and
get to know people different from ourselves, and the resulting diversity of association is favorable to the development of the individual and the hope of a unified society.

The book caught on in both hemispheres, indicat-
ing that the course of urban development worldwide

leaves much to be desired. The reception of that book prompted two others as my ideas about community continued to develop. *Celebrating the Third Place* (2001) is a reader in which proprietors of nineteen places that serve to bring people together in happy communion describe their establishments. The book before you focuses on those places that serve alcoholic beverages, on alcohol's effect in generating social capital, on its connection with conversation and creativity, and on its role in bringing people together.

Most of the manuscript for this book sat in my filing cabinet for over a decade, as I had reservations about its reception. A book promoting the consumption of alcoholic beverages is certain to elicit a good deal of hostile criticism in some circles of our culture. I no longer care about that. Furthermore, research is now abundantly on my side, and books encouraging the prudent consumption of alcohol have long since been in print. The groundbreaker, Dr. Morris Chafetz, produced *Liquor: The Servant of Man* in 1965; Gene Ford's *The French Paradox & Drinking for Health* came out in 1993; and Andrew Barr's *Drink: A Social History of America* appeared in 1999. There are more recent books, but I count these as my favorites.

The reader might well ask herself, given those titles, why another book in favor of the consumption of ethanol? Aside from the fact that the content here is decidedly different, so is the tone. I have endeavored to entertain as much as to edify. While my previous books provoked barely any criticism, this one may well reap a harvest of it, as I am promoting the habitual use of moderate amounts of alcohol—and this is the United States, where the good that alcohol does is still pretty well hidden from view in favor of scaring everyone about the danger of its abuse.

I am a sociologist by training and thus in a field in which one's personal experiences may have an effect on one's course of inquiry. They certainly did in mine. After graduate school I took on teaching positions in small, friendly towns where my wife and I could walk to restaurants, grocery stores, and even, at the University of Nevada at Reno, casinos. We only used the car for such occasions as gem hunting on weekends or trips to California. All the necessities of life were within walking distance, as they had been in the little town where I grew up.

Yet when we moved to Pensacola, Florida, a city plagued by sprawl, we found ourselves for the first time in a modern suburban subdivision. Here, one's house was all-important because there was nothing but houses. Alleys had been done away with, so cars and garages were parked out in front and not attractive. The sidewalks were empty and there were few signs of life, as people seemed to be holed up in their houses.

Mandated setbacks required lengthy but useless front lawns, expensive to maintain. The "use value" of acreage surrounding our house was zero. With nothing within walking distance, we needed two cars even before we had children. The home-to-work shuttle was my life and I hated it. On the drive to work one day, I noticed a bakery with a coffee counter and several picture windows, through which I saw working men having coffee. The next day, I left home early and stopped by. After my third visit, all the men knew and accepted me. There were nine "regulars," and only two of them were in the same line of work. The chatter was rich and the laughter frequent—I never had a completely bad day after that.

On the work front, the lack of community where we lived affected me deeply enough that I abandoned the specialty known as "symbolic interaction" for which I had been trained. One of its major tenets was that reality is a matter of how we define it—what we agree upon in our discussions. The modern American automobile suburb took me away from that view totally. There is a physical reality in which we exist that has a profound effect on what is possible for us.

The deprivation attending life in the automobile suburb prompted the publication of *The Great Good Place*, in which I introduced the simple concept of the "third place," a place apart from home and work where people can get together to enjoy one another's company. Those places—corner groceries, drugstores and their soda fountains, diners, and taverns—made neighborhoods into communities where people got to know one another, where they fit in and enjoyed the social support that such community offers.

Often, when I began to describe my idea about a third place to people, they would immediately say, "Oh, you mean a tavern!" The sociable consumption of alcohol adds another dimension to community. Morris Chafetz called alcohol the "servant of mankind" and goes on to say that it "barely, any longer, serves us as it has for centuries. It brought us together, from all walks of life, in drinking establishments, those perfect democracies where all were equal and in which alcohol set a mood of happy relaxation amid friendly company." In her fine essay "Tavern Talk: The Decline of Political Discourse," Jacqueline Pfeffer Merrill observes that "we don't mix anymore."

While consumption rates for alcoholic beverages in the United States have changed little since the end of World War II, the amount consumed in bars, taverns, and restaurants has dropped significantly. Since the 1970s, our taverns have been in steady decline, and most of us now take our politics and our drinks at home. The tavern is a failing institution, and even the recent rise in niche joints like brewpubs and mixology bars has not helped much, since they too often replace, rather than invigorate, the neighborhood bars that generally serve a different clientele.

The isolation imposed upon us by bad urban planning, and by our own bad habits of sitting in front of the TV, seeks remedy. We are social animals after all, and research has shown that we are happiest among friends. My aim, here, is to encourage the reader to find a place and a time of day to get together with people face-to-face on a regular basis. If it's just for coffee, OK, but that won't do what alcohol can.

Unlike my earlier books, this one does not follow scholarly format. Citations are in the text, and there are no footnotes. Finally, because books dealing with the use of alcohol are typically heavy and admonishing, I've tried to make this one entertaining as well as edifying. My intention, after all, is for everyone to have a good time.

## Tippling and Community

Our economy depends on a high rate of competitive acquisition of things we don't really need but are conditioned to want. Both the corporate world and our government, at all levels, have thus done their utmost to create a "consumer society," a culture hostile to community and the pleasure people derive from the company of others. For the most part, they have succeeded. Looking at the built environment since World War II, the architect Raymond Curran described it as an "Open Order" that affords "a new freedom and a new life style." Its chief characteristics, he notes, are "a high level of mobility, personal isolation, and independence from a communal context."

The most obvious community-killing strategy imposed in the United States has been single-use zoning (that is, laws that prohibit businesses from operating close to where people live, blanket prohibitions that ban not only noisy or polluting establishments but only small shops and taverns). Places where people might meet and get to know one another in residential neighborhoods are now against the law. The "place on the corner" where Americans once got together is today just another private dwelling; nor do we meet afoot, as suburbanites have to get into the car for everything.

In our daily newspaper, there is the "Home of the Week," pictured in color, and its features are glowingly reported. Never is the use value of the surrounding area mentioned. The use value of a neighborhood refers to such beneficial facilities as drugstores, grocery stores, and barber shops that are accessible without the need to drive to them. As Raymond Curran duly noted in *Architecture and the Urban Experience*, homes are homes wherever they are, and what separates one city from another is the quality of the (surrounding) public domain and the experiences it offers (or denies). Most American homes are now located where there is no public domain. Our post-war suburbs are rigged for the boredom that encourages shopping.

Some years ago in Fort Walton Beach, Florida, a Canadian couple with no children bought a modest frame house in an old but quiet neighborhood. When at the bank, during closing, their financial standing became clear, the bank people were aghast—this couple could afford so much more, and every effort was made to get them to come to their senses, to no avail. The house they purchased was one block from an old neighborhood tavern that they visited regularly at day's end and spent time having a couple of beers and chatting with the locals. That couple opted for community.

Let's relate the choice of residential location to the desideratum of happiness or joy and its sources. In the early nineties, two psychologists, Michael Argyle and Maryanne Martin, surveyed a variety of studies to come up with the seven major sources of joy. Here they are arranged in order of importance:

1. Social contact with friends or others in close relationships
2. Sexual activity
3. Success, achievement

4. Physical activity, exercise, sport
5. Nature, reading, music
6. Food and drink
7. Alcohol

Did you notice that television is not on the list, and that is what people depend on so heavily if all they have is a house in their neighborhood? While TV makes the isolation more bearable, it also mitigates against community. Apart from the time not spent with friends, the tirades of the hate-mongers who continually discount and disparage the major media have caused major rifts between those who believe them and those who don't. Even families have been torn apart as questions of what is true depend heavily upon one's viewing habits.

Highly stratified neighborhoods lacking a public life are detrimental to the development of the individual. In order to grow and develop, we all need to meet and interact with a diversity of people. In small communities, that diversity is built into daily life, but in large cities the number of strangers can be bewildering, and the tendency to associate with people much like oneself is strong. Aware of that problem, social worker and organizational consultant Mary Parker Follett, way back in 1918, rested her hopes on the residential neighborhood that, in her day, was not as socially stratified as they are today. She valued her next-door neighbor, who didn't have a college education, and belittled the otherwise highly regarded "cosmopolitans" (or "cosmopolites" as sociologist dubbed them). These are people regarded as free from local prejudices and local attachments and said to be "at home all over the world." Follett declared them to be "all alike." "They know life," she wrote, "across but not down—it's a horizontal civilization, not a vertical one."

Single-use zoning has subsequently destroyed the kind of neighborhoods on which Follett had pinned her hopes. The Supreme Court ruled in favor of the corporate chains, by denying the mom-and-pop stores once common in residential neighborhoods. People would have to drive to large grocery chains for their food. The economy may have benefited from the greater expenses in shopping, but people didn't. They were too much alone.

Newcomers to our country, from Asia to Europe to south of the border, are acutely aware of the lack of community in our residential neighborhoods. Missing their wet markets, hawker centers, local pubs, cafés, and church communities, they may well live for years in our country and, as one of our friends commented, "still feel more of a foreigner than in any other place in the world. . . . People here are proud to live in a 'good' area, but to us these so-called desirable areas are like prisons. There is no contact between households, we rarely see the neighbors and certainly do not know any of them."

But we hardly need to call on foreign visitors to point out the shortcomings of suburban life in the United States. Since the 1990s, there has been a "back-to-the-city movement," especially along the two coasts, by the young and affluent, many of whom grew up in the suburbs, and it has transformed the culture, affordability, and lifeways of city neighborhoods. Unfortunately, this has often led to displacement of the urban poor and the local businesses that served them, resulting in streets dotted with high-end coffee shops that serve as second offices for those working remotely on their laptops. Looking for community and the excitement of city life, these transplants increasingly found themselves living in a parallel manner among their own kind, in neighborhoods that had lost their authentic gathering places.

In some communities, the church and the library have made adjustments in response to the need people have to get together. Churches no longer favor locations along the interstate where land is cheaper—it's too far from where parishioners live. Also, their "fellowship halls" have become larger and more prominent, as getting together after service has become more important. Libraries, once places of silence, still have a quiet room or two, but most of their space invites conversation and group learning, comfortable seating, and room for public presentations; and staff are more likely to be helping patrons on the floor rather than stuck behind a desk or counter.

As our population is increasingly leaving the lifeless suburbs to live downtown or near it, we find increasing need for those two liquids that do more, on a daily basis, to bring strangers together in pleasant and relaxing circumstances than any other public or semi-public facilities. I refer to coffee (minus the laptops) and alcohol; and the tavern, particularly, has no competitor in terms of its capacity to unite people. Wolfgang Schivelbusch, in his chapter on "Drinking Places" (see his book *Tastes of Paradise* [1992]), opens with this sentence: "Throughout history drinking alcohol has meant creating social bonds," and he goes on to explain the unique character of taverns or pubs as we who study them well recognize:

> Although the bar is typically populated by strangers, interaction is available to all who choose to enter. The physical door through which one enters a drinking establishment is a symbolic door as well, for those who come through it declare by entering that unless they put forth evidence to the contrary, they will be open for conversation

with unacquainted others for the duration of their stay.

Unfortunately, it is rare for city government to recognize the good that taverns do for a city, as officials are typically infused with what sociologist Joseph Gusfield called the "malevolence assumption" toward places that sell alcoholic beverages. Take the case of Chicago, which once had about 10,000 taverns. By 1990, it was down to 3,300, and today the number remains fairly stable at about 1,200. Mayor Richard Daley and his son, the second Mayor Richard Daley, made it their cause to shut them down. Today, Chicago is notorious for a crime rate that is much higher than the national average, especially in regards to violent crime. Am I amiss in suggesting that the lack of places where people can "let off steam" has something to do with the violence? When I studied all the bars of Superior, Wisconsin, there were eighty-four of them serving 28,000 people. In Chicago, one ward has two bars to serve 84,000 people.

In a nation with a high rate of residential mobility, coffee shops and especially taverns are very useful places for newcomers to meet locals and learn their way around by talking to them. The disappearance of taverns retards their integration into their own neighborhoods. The journalist Andrew Barr, who wrote the lengthy and thoroughly researched book *Drink: A Social History of America* (1999), expressed his regret at our nation's inability to avail itself of the good that alcohol and the places serving it can contribute. On the last page of the book he writes:

> In retrospect, white Anglo-Saxon Protestant America should have been able to learn from those immigrants and their lack of alcohol-related problems, and should have freed themselves from their tendency to oscillate between drunkenness and abstinence by adopting the habit of drinking wine in regular and moderate quantities with their meals. But it has been an American tendency to regard the consumption of wine, like other alcoholic drinks, as a secretive vice rather than sociable conduct; to see drinking only in terms of the problems that have been associated with it, while ignoring its social values—as a means of sharing, of cementing friendship, of establishing loyalty, of entering adulthood, of declaring freedom.

From 2004 to 2014, more than ten thousand neighborhood bars went out of business in the United States. During that period, one in every six of them closed. The neighborhood bar is dying out, and the camaraderie it offered to so many will not be found elsewhere. The local bar offered an experience of community in a world that no longer does.

And lest readers think that the new lenience given in some states to recreational marijuana use may lead to the same sort the sociability found in bars and taverns, a study conducted at Johns Hopkins University School of Medicine in the 1980s showed that marijuana had a negative effect on the verbal interaction of subjects in a controlled setting. Even herded together in laboratory room, the subjects chose not to relieve the boredom by talking with each other!

The joy of tippling, on the other hand, the cause for which I'm writing and advocating, is most often experienced among the regulars of neighborhood bars. There's far more conversation than drinking there, and it takes place among people from different walks of life who take pride in their diversity. To see this all passing away, and too often to the delight of city governments, makes me wonder about the kind of society we are becoming.

# 2

# *What Is Tippling?*

Dictionaries sometimes differ on the meaning of words, so those who employ them have to pick and choose among the definitions. So it is with *tipple*. I'll not waste time with definitions that differ from the one I want but simply give the first one I found online: "Use the word *tipple* when you want to show that someone drinks moderately but regularly." A tippler, therefore, is someone who drinks habitually but moderately. The word *tipple* may have come from the Norwegian word *tipla*, which means to drink slowly.

We tipplers well outnumber those who abuse alcohol, but it is those unfortunates who command all the attention and shape American thought about the meaning of alcohol in society and in the lives of

individuals. A substantial portion of our population can see no good in alcohol at all. They have much to learn if only they would. We tipplers combine the moderate consumption of alcoholic beverages, camaraderie, and conversation with such delightful results that, for us, tippling has become one of life's most important rituals. With the moderate use of beer, wine, or spirits, we associate friendship, laughter, relaxation, and rejuvenation. In our appreciation of those happy hours and in our ability to hold our own conversationally and otherwise, we are unanimous. All members of our amorphous community are at home in whatever corner of the world some noble publican has anticipated our desires.

The role that tippling can play in informal public life derives from the synergism that occurs whenever alcoholic beverages are shared in dedicated places like taverns and pubs. Synergism (from the Greek *synergos*, or "working together") refers to the cooperative action that yields a greater effect than the sum of individual activities. The talking and imbibing that unfold in a tavern are such that one improves the other. The art of tippling is learned in the company of those who choose to combine it with a bit of palaver—for just as conversation is enhanced by a drink or two, the artful game of conversation moderates consumption of liquor.

Many people are unfamiliar with tippling, and when I begin to explain, they will ask, "Why not just say 'drinking'?" Because as any former virgin knows, it is how we do things that makes the difference. "Drinking" is inaccurate in this context because it includes the binges of college students, the closeted nipping of the alcoholic, the all-day soaking of the idle rich, and other abuses of the privileged. "Drinking" has also acquired a negative connotation in our culture as evidenced by the title of Pete Hamill's bestseller, *A Drinking Life* (1994). Drinking is therein associated not with the great majority who use alcohol responsibly and with good effect, but instead with a man who terribly abused alcohol and himself. "A Drunken Life" would have been a more accurate title, but our culture and those who shape it have long since blurred the distinction between drinking and drunken.

How much alcohol does a tippler consume during any one sitting? What, exactly, is moderation? In *Liquor: The Servant of Man* (1965), Morris Chafetz writes, "Curiously, moderate drinking is beyond definition, yet everybody knows what it is." The US scientific community claims to know, and they spell it out thusly:

1. No more than three to four drinks per episode;
2. No more than twelve to fourteen drinks a week for men, and no more than nine a week for women;
3. Keeping your blood alcohol content (BAC) below 0.055 (0.08 is the driving-while-impaired [DWI] limit nationwide).

The problem with such specifications is that people differ significantly from one another when it comes to how much alcohol they can consume short of getting "tipsy" or "getting a buzz on." It also depends on the rate at which alcohol is consumed over time. Regular or "practiced" drinkers know their limit, and observing it becomes part of the habit of drinking. They would find overindulgence embarrassing to themselves and to their companions. Millions drink responsibly without giving it a thought, as evidenced by the fact that bars the nation over are daily filled with tipplers who remain in control of themselves and need no looking after. And for tipplers, imbibing is always subordinate to its senior partner and raison d'être: talking. When this balance is interrupted by excessive drinking, the first sign of impairment is slow or garbled or confused speech, after all, exactly the opposite of what we're looking for as happy and sociable tipplers.

In China, alcohol is always enjoyed in a social setting, whether among friends, for the sake of rituals, or during long, drawn-out wedding banquets. Enviably, it even plays a role in the business world and is thought to maintain cordial relations between both supervisors and their employees, and among colleagues. Overindulgence is a problem, alas, but public intoxication brings shame to the entire group and is certainly frowned upon.

One can tipple alone, of course, but in doing so, the joy is lost. This is a fact not well understood in our society. In the grips of neo-puritanism, abetted by slanted science, most Americans see the alcohol and not the engaging company in which it is consumed. The community-building camaraderie typically escapes notice, and the drinking is exaggerated. Maurice

Gorham, the Englishman, once made a study of tipplers and found their alcoholic intake to be modest:

> Nothing much is demanded of [the tippler] except to come regularly and show himself to be interested. He need not even drink very much. Most of the regulars are leisurely, even reluctant drinkers. They make a half-pint last a surprisingly long time.

As the anti-alcohol people characteristically paint with too broad a brush, they often accuse tipplers of shortcomings common among less disciplined imbibers. For that reason, the following facts are set forth lest tipplers be confused with lesser beings:

- It is not true that tipplers drink to forget; but neither, of course, do they forget to drink.
- Tipplers are not hard drinkers. They invariably report that it is very easy for them.
- Tipplers are, for the most part, careerists; many of them also have jobs of some sort.
- Tipplers are not driven to drink by their spouses. Usually they supply their own transportation to and from the taproom or are so transported by fellow tipplers.
- Tipplers have no addiction to the beverages they consume; rather, they display an admirable loyalty

to certain products of the brewing and distillation industries.

- Tipplers are never intoxicated or drunken. Sometimes, however, they are over-served.

Levity aside, when tipplers are looked at without prejudice, one finds that conversation is more important than the alcohol. Camaraderie outdistances consumption. As the sales of alcoholic beverages have shifted from the tavern to the home, more people do tipple alone, but that has never been their preference. That our residential neighborhoods disallow bars, that drinking in bars has become far more costly, that we feel more at ease at home and alone—these factors and others pick away at the finest kind of tippling in places created for it. The real joy is communal and should take place in dedicated spaces, such as taverns, pubs, and, yes, bars!

# 3

## *Tippling and Conversation*

The American language seems to contain more euphemisms for drunkenness than for any other word, yet none to describe effects pleasant to the drinker and to those who share his or her company. Correspondingly, American research institutes and centers studying the use of alcohol ignore the positive aspects of alcohol consumption and focus entirely on its abuse. Our language and our scientific research thereby discourages the use of alcohol; and that's a pity, for alcohol, moderately consumed, is one of humankind's greatest inventions and greatest blessings.

It was the noted French chef Vicomte de Mauduit who identified five levels of intoxication: jocose, bellicose, lachrymose, comatose, and *morotose*. Though the word morotose is not found in our language, its meaning is clear both by its Latin root and its coming at the end of this list.

The condition *The Joy of Tippling* pays tribute to is obviously the jocose one; and "merry" or "euphoric" describe this state just as well. H. L. Mencken in writing his essay "Portrait of an Ideal World" argued that people are at their best when "gently stewed," which is a lovely way to put it.

Alcohol encourages conversation just as it arouses the "social impulse" or promotes "social enthusiasm" in the individual. Two centuries ago, the esteemed Dr. Samuel Johnson took note of the fact that, before the wine flowed, conversation was largely confined to those who were good at it while those "conscious of their inferiority" had the modesty not to talk. After drinking, however, they lost their modesty and became "impudent and vociferous." Johnson was probably wrong in attributing loud talking to the wine. As the wine flows, as timidity or reserve fades, more people talk more of the time; they talk more spontaneously, and they must talk more loudly to be heard.

In 1987, Bodil Lindfors and Ralf Lindman, two Scandinavian psychologists, wondered whether acquaintance or alcohol would prompt more talk among groups of four people. Two groups of strangers given alcohol were compared with two groups of people who knew one another and had no alcohol. There was more verbal activity and more self-disclosure among the strangers than among the acquaintances when all four groups discussed a film topic. Alcohol's abetment of social ease is undeniable.

Like the old geezers nursing their coffee, tipplers are often regarded as "solving the problems of the world," or most of them anyway. Religion is avoided as a topic of conversation, and politics has become extremely touchy thanks to the hate-mongers on television and the internet. But sports, news events, the jerks at work, the price of gasoline, the ordeals of air travel, and our dismal and over-paid Congress are sure to be revisited. This is not to say that barroom talk is all lightweight stuff or the airing of grievances. The newspaper columnist Mike Royko, who logged more than enough hours to judge the content, wrote a tribute to such confabulation: "Universities are supposed to be symbols of open thought and discussion. But you can find more of openness and enlightenment in your neighborhood saloon."

I've also found that local matters are more likely to be discussed here, surely because this topic appeals to the interest of everyone, and there are few other places to get the lowdown on the neighborhood. But this is not the evening news or a city council meeting. In the taverns especially, the general discussion may begin with all due attention to some subject, but before you know it, ad hominem remarks break out, and the topic of conversation is subverted to the fun the speakers poke at one another. Issues introduced in all seriousness become the starting point for the display of wit, personality, and good fellowship.

The pleasures of "tippletalk," as I like to call it, derive in part from the number in the group. As this number grows, the laughter increases and the "Lebowitz principle" sets in. This term comes from the literary raconteur Fran Lebowitz who observed that the opposite of talk is not listening—it's waiting. The more people in the group, the longer each individual has to wait to contribute and the more people are listening to what an individual has to say. The degree of hierarchy one may find in the gang at the bar depends on who best contributes to the conversation.

When it comes to banter, people generally have little patience with one another, and when "the boys at the bar" have come to enjoy the best part of the day, patience is smaller still. The chap who prattles on in committee meetings is given no such latitude here. There is less tolerance of bores in men's drinking groups than in most conversational settings. Where more is expected of conversation, or where conversation is expected to be more entertaining, the bore is most resented.

How alcohol affects the quality of these conversations is a complex matter. The relaxed demeanor and obvious enjoyment with which those in drinking groups talk to one another can be deceptive, for it isn't a skill that comes naturally. Like skiing, it's easy if one has done enough of it. It is, in fact, a game, and one wherein the "ball" is passed quickly, held briefly, and the speaker is expected to score.

Though tippling is the junior partner in the synergism between tippling and talking, it is drinking that is crucial because it marks the occasion. One can strike up a conversation anywhere, but tippling requires a staged setting. In social terms, it must be ritualized. There must be beverages, the equipment to concoct them, someone kind enough to serve them, and seating for everyone—and all of this in a place apart. And for synergism to occur, this needs to happen on a regular basis. Most importantly, it must take place among friends, or friendly acquaintances. I'm not talking, of course, about what happens in the cliquish BYOF (Bring Your Own Friend) tavern or bar, where people come in tight groups and give nary a glance to another soul (in fact, many of these groups seem more fixated on their smart phones than the friends they walked in with). Taverns and pubs should regularly attract a number of people who are already friendly acquaintances, and it should encourage friendship among those who first meet in its premises.

As for timing and convenience, a twilight hour after work at a neighborhood or downtown tavern works best, and I am not talking here about that marketing ploy known as "Happy Hour" during which drinks, and often appetizers as well, are offered at reduced prices in order to draw more customers. These events too often lead to overindulgence or "binge drinking" and, for that reason, they are now against the law in some states and in some countries.

While the content of conversation in drinking groups does not differ appreciably from that in other informal gatherings, the manner of expression is typically more demonstrative, more emotional and even more dramatic. As to topics, there is no set agenda and the opportunities to amuse and be amused are fleeting in the extreme. The pace of talk, and its twists and turns, demand more alertness than casual conversation. Correspondingly, the laughs come quicker. Among groups newly formed, a change of topics will occur after several meetings. In the passage of time, the members will talk less about institutional matters and more about themselves. As this happens, as the members get to know one another better, camaraderie grows and friendships are formed.

What I've tried to describe here is that which the German sociologist and philosopher Georg Simmel (1858–1918) called "pure sociability." Human beings,

he argued, have an "impulse to sociability" which means that they often get together for no purpose, duty or role. In these get-togethers, Simmel observed, they feel "joy, vivacity and relief" and when alcohol adds euphoria to that threesome, sociability is at its best—you can tell it in their talk.

# 4

# *Is Tippling Healthful?*

While enjoying said community and the bonhomie found in the third place tavern, the tippler might begin to wonder about his or her long-term health. University of Texas psychologist Dr. Charles Holahan and his six-member team conducted a longitudinal study some years ago following 1,824 people aged fifty-five to sixty-five for a period of twenty years. The sample included moderate drinkers, heavy drinkers, and abstainers. After those twenty years, 41 percent of the moderate drinkers had died, 60 percent of the heavy drinkers had died, and 69 percent of the abstainers had died. The most shocking finding is that the heavy drinkers outlived the abstainers, but from the tippler's point of view, the best news is that we moderate drinkers outlive everybody. As to why those who drink have this advantage, the researchers suggested that "alcohol lubricates so many social interactions, and social interactions are vital for maintaining mental and physical health."

A more recent finding is that friends are vital to longevity. Family is important, of course, but it is the number of friends, not family, that correlates with longevity. This is not necessarily good news for Americans, as research shows that, as time passes, the average American has fewer close friends than he once did. The more Americans experience isolation, the more we tout individualism, and, as the Dominican theologian Father Charles Bouchard observed, it's a type of individualism "that does not sit well with anything that smacks of the common good." Recognizing that fact, Kathryn Nelson of the now defunct Danforth Foundation, which distributed grants to such causes as downtown revitalization and neighborhood redevelopment, wrote this: "In the celebration of individualism, what is lost is the celebration of how we're all in this together. What is lost is the equally important concept of community."

In lieu of community, which never depended on a single individual, the individual can cultivate a "network." Networks are not, as many of my colleagues see them, a superior form of community. That's the bias of modern American individualism. All real communities exist in a place; they are place-bound. Networks constitute the efforts of an individual to find the care, concern, and comfort characteristic of community in regular association with friends. For tipplers the reward is twofold: the joy of regularly spending time in good company and a longer life.

A summary report from Harvard on the risks and benefits of alcohol suggests that it is both a tonic and a poison and that the difference is "mostly in the dose." Moderate drinking has many beneficial effects, while heavy drinking poses a great many risks. There is a difference of opinion, however, on what constitutes moderate drinking. The National Institute of Alcohol Abuse and Alcoholism (NIAAA) defines the limit as three to four drinks a day for men and two to three drinks a day for women. The Department of Health and Human Services, the Department of Agriculture, and the Mayo Clinic define moderate drinking as one drink a day for women and two a day for men. Though there is no universal agreement on what constitutes a drink (or a "unit"), the above-mentioned organizations all agree that it consists of a 12-ounce beer, 5 ounces of wine, or 1.5 ounces of 80-proof distilled spirits.

It has been suggested that the limits set on moderate drinking, and thereby on heavy drinking, are puritanical. For example, the weekly limit set by NIAAA, the most "generous" of the four organizations, is fourteen drinks a week for men and seven for women. Research has shown that for "heavy drinkers" to reach that level of excess, which makes their longevity equal to those who don't drink, they'd have to consume about thirty drinks a week. In that light, the heavy drinkers who outlived the abstainers may not, for the most part, be that "heavy" after all.

Studies show the elderly are increasingly social, more friendly, and alert with moderate alcohol consumption—a little tippling, that is. One study showed one to two ounces of whiskey preferable to either diazepam (Valium) or pentobarbital in putting elderly dentistry patients at ease. Another study showed that the elderly had increased morale, worried less, slept better, and showed cognitive improvement with two drinks a day containing only 0.4 ounce of alcohol. Of course, the therapeutic benefits of alcohol are not limited to the elderly, as Richard Klein, professor emeritus of French literature, duly noted in his 2010 essay for the *Chronicle Review*, "The Case Against Health":

For many people, a life without the oil of drink becomes too much to bear. A little wine eases the vague and subcutaneous unease that stress puts on our muscles; a martini induces a moment of forgetfulness when the anxieties and fears of the day recede. In pursuit of happiness, Americans are insistently encouraged to consume vast quantities of anti-anxiety drugs and antidepressants, but booze is never publicly celebrated. Rarely do we hear about the charms and benefits of alcohol, or the sociability it has promoted from the dawn of time, or the pleasure and consolation it has infused into the lives of billions over the course of human history.

The health benefits claimed for alcoholic beverages are different for beer, wine, and distilled spirits and will be discussed in that order. Beer is sometimes referred to as "liquid bread" due to its high calorie count. A slice of white bread has 79 calories, while a slice of whole wheat has 128. A regular twelve-ounce beer has 145 or 153 calories, while my favorite has 250 calories, and Sierra Nevada's Bigfoot has a whopping 330 calories. The reader can understand why we don't get wine or whiskey bellies, while beer bellies are quite common.

On the positive side, beer drinkers have a 31 percent lower risk of heart disease than nondrinkers. That's because beer contains HDL (the "good cholesterol") in ample supply. A compound found in the hops used in making beer is said to help inhibit the enzymes that produce cancer, and beer drinkers get twice as much vitamin B6 as wine drinkers; B6 helps

the body fight off disease and increases brain function-
ing and energy. Beer is rich in antioxidants that reverse
cellular damage; it also lowers blood pressure. Unique
to beer among the alcoholic beverages is the fact that
those who drink it have 40 percent fewer kidney stones
than those who don't. Moderate drinkers are also are
less likely to develop type 2 diabetes.

To maximize the positive effects beer may have on
the body, one should consume only one or two bottles
a day. Since beer may be consumed all day long at the
rate of one bottle per hour, many people exceed that
amount. Beer is, after all, the third most popular drink
in the world after water and tea.

Wine wins the longevity contest, for those who
drink wine live, on average, four years longer than
those who drink beer or distilled spirits. I suppose
that's because those who drink it tend to have more
education and more money, but wine does have impressive physiological advantages. Wine drinkers,
for example, have a 52 percent lower chance of developing prostate cancer, and a 45 percent lower
chance of developing colon cancer. The possibil-
ity of a stroke is about 50 percent less among wine
drinkers than among nondrinkers. Wine drinkers are
43 percent less likely to develop cataracts than beer
drinkers and 32 percent less than nondrinkers. Wine
drinkers are also 30 percent less likely to have a heart

attack than nondrinkers. The polyphenols in wine help regulate blood sugar in the body, and the procyanidins in red wine result in a lower rate of heart disease.

The French experience with wine is its strongest testimony. The French eat a high-fat diet, including all manner of rich foods; they smoke cigarettes; and they don't jog. They drink an average of sixteen gallons of wine per person each year compared to our two gallons per person in the United States. Yet the rate of heart disease in France is less than half of ours (143 per 100,000 versus 315 per 100,000), and they live an average of two and a half years longer than we do.

Their most popular wine is red, which contains piceatannol, a stilbenoid that inhibits the formation of fat cells. They shop daily for fresh foods, which are better for the body than the multitude of processed foods with which we hurriedly stuff ourselves. It is not surprising that the oldest recorded living person, Jeanne Calment, was a product of this culture. She was born on 21 February 1875 and died on 4 August 1997—that's 122 years and 164 days, and she drank wine every day of her adult life. It wasn't the usual red, but a fortified port of about 20 percent alcohol by volume (ABV). When interviewed, she said she did nothing to prolong her years but that a sense of humor seemed to help. She took up fencing at age eighty-five and continued to ride her bicycle until she reached one hundred years of age.

In China, as the living standards of people improved over the last thirty years, especially in urban areas, their concern for both their health and the status of their drinks also increased. *Baijiu*, their powerful "white" spirit, is still considered the "national drink," but wine and beer consumption is growing rapidly. China imports the top-grade brands and produces respectable domestic varieties that are gaining notice overseas.

But let's not downplay distilled spirits, which have more health benefits than one might image. Distilled spirits, generally, reduce stress, decrease the incidence of heart disease, and aid the circulatory system. Those appear to be the major benefits. Here are just a few more: whiskey, taken straight, is your best drink for dieting, with no carbohydrates and only ninety-six calories; Scotch has even less, with seventy-eight calories and no carbs. Whiskey also has ellagic acid in it, which stops DNA contact with cancer-causing compounds. Gin reduces joint inflammation and eases the pain of arthritis. Rum increases the mineral density of bones, which helps prevent osteoporosis.

Just as important, how does alcohol make people feel? Psychologists tell us that low and moderate amounts of alcohol make it easier to show affection and put us in a more sociable mood. Tippling also reduces tension and makes us less self-conscious. Whereas moderate amounts of alcohol reduce the occurrence of depression, it's not surprising that heavy amounts have the opposite effect. Alcohol, in low or moderate amounts, makes us feel pleasant and carefree. Researchers have also demonstrated that alcohol improves certain kinds of cognitive function, such as short-term memory and problem-solving ability.

Early in this discussion, I mentioned the bias of individualism. I have an opposing social bias in that I believe that getting together with friends on a regular basis is essential to one's health, both mental and physical. Since alcohol and the places that serve it, and do so publically, facilitate and encourage those meetings, this may be the most important benefit that alcohol bestows. Beyond any "maybes," the basic health fact remains: moderate drinkers live longer than heavy drinkers or abstainers. So let's move on to enjoying those extra years by finding the best places to drink and converse.

# 5

## *The Noble Tradition*

---

In regards to Prohibition, which lasted from 1920 to 1933, Bob Brown, a writer and member of New York's bohemian scene, wrote, "All over the civilized world, except America, the saloon stands out as a splendid social institution." By the time his book *Let There Be Beer!* came out in 1932, the failed experiment was nearly over. The saloon, even in the United States if you go back far enough, was a splendid institution. Its vital role in building our country is all but forgotten now. A good saloon keeper, said Toots Shor, the legendary restaurateur, is the most important man in the community; and when communities still existed in the United States, that was true. In those days, many people kept their money in a saloon keeper's safe because it was deemed more trustworthy than a bank. Also, a man running for political office back then could claim no better credential than having run a good saloon.

In colonial times, the saloon or tavern, which often served meals for the inn above it, was quite literally the center of community life, and many of our country's most civic-minded leaders owned or operated them. These included Samuel Adams, the father of the American Revolution; Ethan Allen, leader of the Green Mountain Boys; John Adams, second president of the United States; William Penn, the founder of Pennsylvania; Andrew Jackson, military hero and seventh president of the United States; and even Abraham Lincoln, who obtained his license in 1833.

When new towns opened on the frontier, the tavern was usually the first structure erected, and it served many functions. They have doubled as courtrooms, auction houses, libraries, hospitals, and places of worship. They have served as military recruitment offices and barracks, settings for theatrical performances, and hospitality headquarters. They have hosted businessmen's meetings and served as "second offices" for politicians, authors, salesmen, and others whose endeavors brought them into contact with the public.

As our big cities were beginning to grow, saloons occupied the prime downtown locations. In time, however, they gave way to big banks and, later, to our huge corporate towers as our "downtowns" became the hectic, cold, and impersonal places we are now at pains to humanize. More than in any other nation, our major cities represented the triumph of commerce over community.

Our taverns were once the true town centers, in which residents got to know one another in the most informal, relaxed, and friendly manner possible, and wherever the vastly reduced number of them still exist, they still perform this function.

I'm going to introduce the reader to several places that I consider the best taverns and pubs I've visited, ones that have made my travels more memorable than the reasons that brought me to their cities. I wish I could guarantee that they haven't changed, but I know that at least some of them have.

Dewey's Ale House in Brattleboro, Vermont, for example, is no longer active. Ray McNeill knew how to manage a great bar: he threw out all the noisy distractions and made it a great place for newcomers to get to know one another. He also served each brand of beer at its optimal temperature. Still active and not far away is Leunig's Bistro & Café in Burlington. When I was there, Dennis Morrisseau was in charge and of the opinion that the only good things in this country came out of bars; accordingly, he presided with a sense of dignity and purpose worthy of the best houses.

There's an Irish pub in San Luis Obispo, California, named McCarthy's after "Red Devil" McCarthy, a one-time professional wrestler. He was in his nineties when I dropped in and was letting young Duffy (only in his eighties) run the place. I asked my friend Peter Apanel about the owner. "You might be able to take him now," Peter opined, "but I'd be wary of any five-foot-seven guy who's shaped like a fire plug." The suds were first rate at McCarthy's.

In my wife's hometown of Duluth, Minnesota, you'll find the Pickwick. Nobody seems to know how it got its name, but for decades it has been the place to which everyone who's left town visits when they return. There are spacious dining rooms, meeting rooms, and a cozy area for evening socializing. My favorite was the bar itself, where everything was just right and supervised at both ends by two glass-encased stuffed white owls. It was wonderful when Steve and Tony Wisocki were in charge, but at my last visit the owls were gone and so was the gemütlichkeit. I hope it will realize its potential again.

Many urban downtown areas are coming back to life, thanks to young entrepreneurs who "don't know any better" and who bring energy, enthusiasm, and vision to their efforts. My good friend "Prish" Moran did it with a coffeehouse in West Buffalo, New York; while in Seattle, three young men (dubbed "The Three Fools") salvaged the Blue Moon tavern from a host of perils.

In Superior, Wisconsin, which is a tremendous bar city (eighty-four of them to serve a population of 28,000 locals plus visitors) there's a gentleman's bar named after Frankie, the owner. Frankie's is popular with some of the publicans who run those noisy establishments the youngsters favor. Frankie determined opening hours according to how many regulars were waiting at the door. If there were more than two, Frankie would come a little earlier the next day. There's no music or gadgetry save for an antique game on legs of some kind just on the left when you enter. Nobody plays it; nobody knows how. It's Frankie's joke, we think.

Nick Klonis's place, Evangelo's, offers a blessed retreat from all the upscale shopping in Santa Fe, New Mexico. Polynesian decor in the middle of the desert may seem a little strange, but the Australian Awesome Wells ranked it thirty-first among his "100 Best Bars in America" in *Barhop USA: One Man's Quest to Find America's Ultimate Bar.* As so much of original Santa Fe has been replaced by what money brings, one hopes Evangelo's will survive as an authentic watering hole amid buildings restored, not as they were, but as they should have been according to the town's consulting experts.

McGovern's in Newark, New Jersey, is one of the town's bright spots, found in the college area and owned by William Scully, whose corned beef is world-class and who keeps the temperature of the Guinness perfect. The service is quick and friendly, and there's no TV to shout ESPN games at the customers, who easily fall into the delightful habit of talking to one another.

When the wealthy folk along our East Coast used to take the train to Florida, Ormond Beach was the end of the line. One of my favorite places there was John Cunningham's Alexander's Café and Bakery, which also served wine, beer, and cocktails. I was impressed with his treatment of Killian's Irish Red—better than I'd ever had it—and his food, including home-made potato chips, was first rate. It was a pleasure to see business-suited women come in, sit at the bar, and be completely "at home." And there was a peaceful and amiable co-existence there between yuppies, old-timers, and people who really work for a living.

All too familiar with bars that fail to survive "improvement," I was heartened by Freddie's 35er Bar in Pasadena, California. At the time of my visit, Jennine Terzo was remodeling and asked me if I thought they should operate in another place across the street for fear of losing customers in the meantime. "Not at all," I told her. It was an easy call. The day before the scheduled opening day, the weather was so nice that the staff propped the doors to let the air in, and within an hour the place was packed. If I recall correctly, it was then the only really complete bar in town.

One can get misty-eyed thinking about places like the Sunnyside Tap in Traer, Iowa. Owner Delbert

Boldt had finally retired last time I passed though, and I believe his daughter and son-in-law had taken over. Iowa's small towns have mostly escaped sprawl and still offer friendly self-contained communities. Some of them even have alcohol-free bars for children. The Sunnyside Tap, like most of Iowa's taverns, is a neat and tidy place, seductive in its appeal. Customers play cards in all the taverns there, and if they invite you over to play Pepper, you might never leave. The journalist Maurice Gorham once said of England's pubs that the new ones may be better, but the old ones are nicer. Iowa's got the nicer ones.

When visiting our nation's capital, I take lodging in Alexandria and ride the Metro into DC. Portner's Tavern, a beautiful achievement in carpentry, was located just off the town's main drag on Saint Asaph Street in Old Town. On my first visit, I recall intruding upon a gentleman, with a handsome Danish pipe in his mouth, reading a book at the bar. He bought me a beer, and before I could reciprocate, my driver arrived, so I took his address and sent him a little gift when I got home. Sometimes you meet people you wish you could be around forever. On another occasion, the dark beer and shrimp hors d'oeuvres, plus the company, were so compelling I stayed a day longer than I'd planned, and got caught in "the storm of the century."

Once in DC, I was directed to Tunnicliff's Tavern on 222 Seventh Street SE, only half a block from a Metro station, and a hangout for politicians and celebrities. There I met restaurateur Lynne Breaux, formerly of New Orleans, who, when "the Big Easy got a little boring," came to DC for the excitement. "Transplanting the joie de vivre of my native city to this politically correct and paranoid town seems to be my life's work," she said. But her life's work would assume much larger proportions, for after three years at Tunnicliff's, she became president of the Restaurant Association of Metropolitan Washington. After a decade of her efforts, the dining scene in DC exploded into prominence.

Molly Malone's is my favorite bar in Los Angeles. I was there once, on St. Patrick's Day, talking to a handsome young lawyer when a bubbling young woman entered, microphone in hand, and headed right for him. "Is this real?" he said. "Yes," she replied, "you are really going to be on radio!" "No," he said, feeling her blouse collar between thumb and forefinger. "Is this really nylon?" She wrapped the cord around the microphone and left immediately.

In San Francisco, I liked O'Doul's, to which I could walk and which had fine choices on tap and tables where you could sit next to strangers and talk like old friends. If you want to enjoy fine tobacco with your beer, try Schmidt's Tobacco and Trading Company, north of San Francisco on Solano Avenue in Albany. It's an old residence that now offers fine ales, good tobacco, and no TV or jukebox, in a homey atmosphere.

I met the complete publican and bar host extraordinaire, Rick Knight, back in the nineties. His place was Holmes and Watson Ltd., located at 450 Broadway in Troy, New York. Rick built a veritable community around that establishment and the myriad activities he sponsored, which were announced in his monthly publication, *The Lestrade Report*. Rick arranged Single Malt Tours and Single Malt Dinners, Bock Beer Tastings, Casting Calls for Sherlock Holmes dramas, Cigar Smokers' Nights, Pipe Smokers' Nights, a dinner on Leslie Nielsen's birthday, Third Tuesday Beer Debuts, Clothe the Kids events, and more. He even gave me the use of his office when I was in town. Rick's community offered occasions and events that kept everyone anticipating the next good time. Eventually, however, the taxes and the politics of the great state of New York drove Rick Knight into another state and another profession. I keep a thick file of his menus and newsletters should I ever meet someone else who wants to go all the way in operating a great bar.

The bars I've mentioned above are all my memory can manage as I write about them now. To me, they have been the "welcoming centers" of their cities.

Our cities bear no resemblance to Paris, as you may well know. They are often too much as pictured, with large, cold buildings between which people hurry along paying no attention to others. Here and there, however, one can still find the friendly tavern, where the stranger can enter and be welcomed into friendly company with no need for formal introductions. The tavern is ideal in this respect because of the mood that prevails within, and for that, we are indebted to alcohol. There is a sense of unity, however, that exceeds the sharing of the same room and even participating in the same activity of tippling. Greetings are extended as the latest arrivals take their place at the bar. Yet there is no urgency to snag a seat, and meandering from one group to the next, sampling the conversation, is but the natural behavior of those who been made to feel at ease.

In her novel *Everybody Rise* (2015), Stephanie Clifford shows an appreciation of that mood when she writes, "I always think the opening moments are the hardest, before everyone has had enough to drink." I am not a fan of the cocktail party, Lord knows, but what you can find in a tavern or pub is a different story. When you enter a friendly tavern, the mood has already been established: the party is waiting for you.

# 6

# *The Tippler's Temple*

---

Places open to the public that serve alcoholic beverages go by many different names but, for our purposes, "bar" will do. As tipplers talk much more than they drink, two criteria are uppermost: Is a given bar a good place to drink? That has to do with quality, menu, cost, and all aspects of service. Second, is a given bar a good place to talk? That has to do with sound, seating, and the capacity of the place to accommodate groups of varying sizes in comfort.

I checked the written word, which is to say writers, for advice about choosing between one bar and another. It is easy for writers to believe that they are experts, and the delusion, no doubt, is fostered by the fact that they work all alone. There's nobody around to question the notions that appear on the pages, and then, as all too often happens, the writer gets his stuff published, and what more proof does one need? Note the similarity between *author* and *authority*.

With the above caveat in mind, let us consider what the "experts" say about how to pick a bar. The first starts out by telling us what a "great" bar really is (show us the way, master!). Turns out a great bar is one that serves the "primary function" of "relieving loneliness, boredom, and dread." Where did he get that idea? Sounds like dangerous advice, as drinking in the condition he describes can lead to addiction.

That risk aside, try to imagine a bar filled with the lonely, the bored, and the dreadful. My mind conjures up people with poor posture wallowing in self-pity to the nasal whining of a Hank Williams wannabe. An evening in company like that and I'd probably be ready to take the pledge. Tippling, as you are tired of my telling you, is supposed to be *fun*.

Another expert tells us to strike out on our own to find a "bar bar," and how do we know when we've found it? Well, most importantly, it's nowhere, which means that if anybody knows you're there, it's not a "bar bar." That fellow seems to suffer from being too well known, or from the illusion that he is too well known. In total contrast, the whereabouts of a genial tippler, when he's not at home or work, is usually not much of a mystery. It's very likely that he's enjoying himself in a place he and his buddies have helped put on the map. If you like to be a loner, however, and the prospect of being mugged doesn't scare you, you may wish to roam the back streets at night in search of that magical destination. Certainly it would be an adventure.

A third "expert" speaks with scientific credentials. He tells us to avoid dimly lit places because reduced lighting generally encourages people to drink. He also warns against places where the seating is primarily in booths as they increase our isolation from other people, and that encourages us to drink. Also, do not drink facing a wall, as that, too, makes us want to drink. Finally, he warns against bars that are noisy, for noise of any kind will make us want to drink.

The ideal bar, then, is one in which we would not be encouraged to have a drink. We are, as the expert points out, easily victimized by a variety of stimuli over which we have little control. Golly Jeepers! What if the bar is owned and operated by an evil man who wants us to drink and thereby increase his profits and he knows that Mummy isn't along to protect us?

A friend of mine with kids in college told me that his son and friends drove to a neighboring city to do their drinking. My curiosity got the best of me. Why not a local bar, I wondered, and I drove over to have a look at that tavern. The place was very quiet: no music, no television. The boys had their favorite booth and they talked and talked. They were unusual for their age, for the general rule is the younger the crowd, the more sound there must be.

But this preference is not limited to youth. There seems to be what might be called an "anti-reflection" aspect to our culture. I began to notice it in a photographers' darkroom in which there was a small white radio that didn't work. Without exception, everyone who came in to use the facilities tried to make that little instrument work. Later, I talked to an assistant to the pastor of a large Lutheran church, which had recently surveyed parishioners to find out if there was anything to be improved in its services. The major complaint was the time devoted to a silent prayer. Finally, our house was, for a time, a "cookie station" for the Girl Scouts, and mothers would often come in and stare around as if something was wrong. There was no TV on!

I'm not surprised, then, that so many people want there to be something "going on" when they enter a bar, even if it's only the illusion of something going on. The bar business harkens to this need. Sports bars generally provide the distractions visually, rather than with sound. In many of them, you'll find more television sets than customers. My choice is always the "gentlemen's bar," where civility reigns and conversation is the main entertainment.

Experience shows that the best bars tend to be those in which Mine Host is also Mine Owner, where customers have direct access to the man or woman in charge. The owner can cater to customer requests as employees cannot. The owner can open earlier if the demand is there. She can order a product presently not on the shelf. He can adjust the televisions set. More importantly, it is in the tipplers' best interests to become friends of the owner, for they well know that they are not his best customers.

For inspiration here we could look to the Old World, where bar owners are not in the business of encouraging compulsive drinking. In France, at least in years past, it was a bistro tradition to serve each drink on a saucer and to remove only the glasses from the table as they were emptied. The saucers accumulated and reminded everyone how many drinks each person had had.

European bars also tend to have more nonalcoholic beverages on offer. The English pub never runs out of ginger beer, orange squash, and Ribena (black-currant juice). France, however, surpasses its neighbors with freshly pressed juices such as *jus de poire, jus de pêche,* or *citron pressé* (lemonade). These offerings temper overindulgence in alcohol and encourage family and friends to join in the fun that tipplers always bring to the table.

Here, however, the bar business is subject to simple arithmetic: the more drinks poured in a given day, the better the profits. Unfortunately, tipplers don't drink enough. As one owner expressed it, "If those guys drank half as much as they chatter, I'd be a rich man." Experienced owners have learned, however, that bar seating that's filled is a better draw than bar seating that's empty, and so relations are generally cordial. It also doesn't hurt to treat the owner to a drink from time to time.

The design of bars is changing. In their heyday, the majority of them were long and narrow places for the simple reason that taxes went up significantly according to the amount of footage taken up on the street. Both front door and back were used, however, with the regulars often taking the alley and parking behind the bar. Those long and narrow places had a feature that more modern bars don't, as the emphasis now is more on curvilinear seating where customers can face one another. That feature was the back bar.

The lengthy bar dictated by the overall shape of the place also meant that there was a great deal of space on the wall behind it, far more than was needed for bottles. The back bar contained both information and entertainment. There was, for example, usually some kind of notification that drinks would not be served on credit. That policy was near universal, for as the tavern owner Sean Mooney pointed out in his *Practical Guide to Running a Pub,* there is a loss of roughly fifty cents on every dollar of credit extended. The manner in which this policy was stated varied considerably. A sign simply stating "No Credit" was common, but the owners often had fun with it, for example: "If You Believe in Credit, Loan Me $5.00." Another version read "Never Drink on an Empty Wallet."

In a bar on Duluth, Minnesota's "wild side," credit was extended to some of the regulars, prompting this sign:

## TO OUR PAST-DUE CUSTOMERS
When you die, please let us be your pallbearers.
We carried you so long, we'd like to finish the job.

Returning to the matter of choosing a bar, I'm reminded that there's a book on the subject in which the author claims that he can tell exactly what a tavern is like by giving the place the once-over from the outside. Now dear tippling friends, I may pull your leg a little from time to time, but I would never go that far! The fact of the matter is that even the most experienced tippler, especially in a strange city, sometimes enters the wrong establishment.

What seems like a pleasant enough oasis may, once you step through the door, reveal itself to be one of the devil's own. Right there on the bar you may spot one of those ten-ounce cans of beer: the undersized brew at an oversized price. You may be about to order when a juke box kicks in at full volume and you are jarred enough to make your spine ripple. Or your ears may be assaulted by some horse's patoot guffawing at his own jokes, or the pathetic mumblings of a bleary-eyed drunk who should have been ousted hours ago. In all such cases and many others, you've stumbled into the wrong place.

What to do about it? For years, I did what I considered the polite thing. I'd have one beer and leave, often without finishing it. I cannot say what flaw in my upbringing caused me to do that but I never liked doing it. I've never enjoyed one of those pro forma pilsners and never felt the house deserved the small profit it garnered from them.

The "improved response" came upon me, as I recall, without my even thinking about it. I'd set foot in an inviting corner bar in St. Louis one afternoon and headed for the mahogany close to where a customer was seated. I gave him a nod and a friendly "How ya doin'?" only to get a cold, fish-eyed stare in return. Instantly I realized that if this was that sorry bastard's kind of place, it wasn't mine, and, as quickly as I was taken aback, my arms extended outward, my eyes rolled heavenward, and I executed a most graceful turn off my left toe and proceeded directly out of there. How nicely, I prided myself, did the choreography fit the situation.

So that's my standard response now, and I recommend it. When it's time to dance the back-step, do it. You mosey into the wrong cantina, do the Wiskalopian Whirl. If the joint is a turn-off, execute the One-Eighty, the Tippler's Turnabout, the Righteous Rotation. Get the heck out of there and find a decent place. Do not insult. Do not try to reform. Just do your trick and leave 'em wondering. That's their just desserts.

Another sort of place to avoid is what I call the BYOF (Bring Your Own Friend) tavern or bar. At first, these might appear as the cozy establishments of which we tipplers are so fond, particularly when they are crowded and the conversation is thrumming. But there is no unity; people enter these places with their own friends or in pairs and stake out their territory. There they cluster, and anyone entering the establishment alone is sure to stay that way. No one meanders or calls out to others across the room—the laughter is not general. The setting here, by the way, is incidental, and if a cushier place opens elsewhere, that's where the patrons will go.

As a final note, I'd like to suggest a way to relate to a bar, especially a local one, that has the potential to become your "home away from home." Just walking in feels good: the decor, the happy faces, the noise control, and the greeting from behind the bar. Here, I would suggest, that you sit at the bar because you don't want the relative privacy that booths allow. You want to be part of what's going on. When you order, buy one for the bartender and you will immediately be a special customer. Some of life's best hours may be spent right here, most enjoyably in the company of different sorts of people and both sexes, as in the next chapter I somewhat boldly attempt to discuss.

# 7

## *The Feminine Touch*

---

Tippling has been a male tradition as long as public drinking establishments existed to host it. But what about women? If the Women's Christian Temperance Union had gotten its way, there would be no female tipplers. Frances Willard, who presided over that body until her death, declared: "Drink and tobacco are the great separatists between men and women. Once they used these things together, but woman's evolution has carried her far beyond them."

But evolution, erelong, became revolution, and in our day, three out of every five women drink alcoholic beverages, if only once a year. More men drink than do women, and men drink more alcohol when they

drink than women do; the latter fact having to do with differences in male versus female physiology.

Men's bodies contain about 10 percent more water than women's bodies, and that lesser amount of fluid means higher concentrations of alcohol in a woman's bloodstream. Also, men have more blood in their bodies because they have more muscle and less fat than women. Muscle has a large amount of blood throughout, while fat has little. Finally, gastric alcohol dehydrogenase, an enzyme that breaks down alcohol, is about 50 percent more abundant in men than in women. Generally speaking, one drink will affect a woman as much as two drinks will for men. Finally, alcohol carries greater health risks for women than for men, especially in regards to damage to the liver and pancreas, and this, in addition to the greater disapproval heaped on intoxicated women, helps explain why 40 percent of women don't drink.

But the majority do and increasingly so. Do they drink in the most proper manner, which is to say, do they tipple? Do they tipple with men? The beloved history professor Madelon Powers, author of *Faces Along the Bar* (1998), cautioned against it. Her argument was that "on the one hand, decent women should be protected from the rough world of men; on the other hand, the rough world of men should be protected from decent women." But not much protection has been necessary. The compatibility between men and women in the barroom has been beautifully documented by author Rosie Schaap in her book *Drinking with Men* (2013). Ms. Schaap found community and her sense of belonging in bars as nowhere else. She is not alone in that, but she is alone in describing her experiences with such skill that the book is pure entertainment.

For most women, accompanying a husband has been the way into barroom tippling, but many husbands prefer male-only tippling. Bonnie, a colleague of mine, was married to one of those, and it frustrated her no end. Finally she took action on her own: calling together close female friends, she explained the situation. She named the little group of willing participants the Tri Mi Pi Sorority, and those ladies often talk and tipple at the tavern of their choice until closing time.

The most impressive stride women are making is in hosting, and their expertise is evident as both bartenders and bar owners. A recent Cornell study found that, as bar owners, women fare better than men. Further, bars owned by women have a higher survival rate in our nation's larger cities. Rande Gerber, co-founder of the Gerber Group back in 1991, which owned more than thirty bars around the world, reported that 85 percent of staff were women. When in charge, they covet input from the staff, they're more flexible in dealing with people, they put women seated at the bar more at ease, and they are often better at cooling down customers who get out of hand.

Following publication of my second book and ensuing travel, I met and became friends with several truly remarkable people devoted to improving the cities in which they lived. They've done it as owner-operators of extremely successful places where people eat, drink, and enjoy themselves in conducive surroundings.

Joyce Goldstein was in her sixth year at the helm of her revolutionary San Francisco restaurant, Square One, when my book came out, and she bought copies for every member of her staff. We began exchanging letters and I invited her to write a piece for *Celebrating the Third Place*. Her sixteen-hour, seven-day-a-week schedule allowed her no time to do it, but she supplied me with a stack of reviews from which I was able to add to what I saw and what she told me, and we managed the publication.

Joyce is a fan of Mediterranean cooking and well-traveled in pursuit of it, taking recipes from Italy, Spain, France, Greece, Turkey, the Middle East, and North Africa. "Square One" was chosen as the name of her restaurant because a new menu appeared every day; a menu almost totally changed from the day before and including over twenty appetizers, entrées, and desserts. Joyce had an open kitchen, and the establishment, overall, was neat as a pin with nothing hidden from view. Over four hundred meals a day were served, and most of her customers were regulars, many of whom were given a friendly call when their favorite dishes were to be served.

Joyce Goldstein was well prepared for the adventure of taking on Square One. She had taught cooking for years, written cookbooks, and gained organizational experience from having managed Alice Waters's famous Chez Panisse restaurant in Berkeley. Joyce absolutely loved cooking and understood, as few restaurant owners seem to, that the taste of the food is the most important thing the house has going for it. In one interview she confided, "Sometimes I'll be standing here and I'll watch a table of customers take their first bites. Suddenly everyone stops talking, sits back, and smiles. Then I know I've given them a delicious present."

Chef Goldstein's restaurant was not only a great place to eat, it was also a great place to drink. As one reviewer observed, if you wanted Scotch on the rocks, you got as generous a serving as you'd pour for yourself at home. But the real treat was in the wines, arguably the best in the city. The fellow in charge of the wine list was Joyce's son Evon, the youngest person ever to pass the exam given by the Court of Master Sommeliers in England. His mother said, "My son, the sommelier, can taste layers in wine as I can taste layers in food."

It was a happy circumstance that Evon, having grown up eating his mother's dishes, was alert to wines that complemented them. He found, for example, that Pinot Noirs were very flexible wines and went so well with so much of her food that his list contained many fine versions of it. At Square One, there was a wine list for each diner, giving everyone a chance to study it well. There were many choices under ten dollars and many more under twenty. In addition, Evon had a special wine list for connoisseurs.

The second restaurateur to bowl me over was Lynne Breaux, whom, as you already know, I met in the nation's capital. After success as a fashion model and managing a deluxe hotel in New Orleans, Lynne decided to move "from a city that played too hard to one that worked too hard." She took over Tunnicliff's Tavern, which dates back to colonial times, gave it new life, and ran it for thirteen years. The place is located on the same hill as the Capitol building, only six blocks away.

That tavern, as described by Ms. Breaux, is "a restaurant, bar, patio, and parlor. . . . It is where politicians, poets, and people of all ages, occupations, and cultures converse, commiserate, collaborate, celebrate, satiate, relate, date, mate, appropriate, and often act inappropriate." The late author Christopher Hitchens, one of her regulars, described her tavern as a place where "you can recline in the company of delinquent congressional staff members, in a special armchair and newspaper-and-music cigar section right off the main bar area."

Lynne Breaux took a degree in sociology from Louisiana State University, and it served her well in the hospitality field. Early on, she wrote a piece about "the five r's"—restaurant begets retail, begets residential, begets resurgence, begets revenue. Would she be surprised to learn, years later, that many malls are saving themselves by adding restaurants? Hardly. She operated Tunnicliff's from 1988 to 2001, the "pre–cell phone era," and she observed what happens to people when they leave the isolation of their dwellings behind for the company of the tavern. She writes:

> Third place aficionados rarely need the classifieds. Regulars and staff walk in, run into long-lost or newfound friends, partake of comfortable conversation and, voilà, a new job, a new membership, romantic or not, a place to live. All because they turned off the TV and the computer and departed from the social isolation of the individual or the couple.

In the blizzard of 1993, during eleven consecutive "snow days," Tunnicliff's was packed with people who, in their ensuing camaraderie, beat the weather while nearby "NoVaps" (Northern Virginia people) were stuck in their homes playing with their isolating electronics. When, in the January brownout of 1995, the mayor ordered the closing of all nonessential businesses, the tavern owners on Capitol Hill got together and decided that they were essential. "Customers called in a panic to see if we'd be open, and we were, much to the relief of our regulars," Lynne wrote. "So instead of hundreds of individual ovens, heaters, and television sets wasting thermal units, everyone congregated in just a few watering holes, conserving energy and having a ball. Ah, the unwitting irony of government—we are indeed an essential business."

Lynne Breaux bemoaned the low level of respect for waiters, bartenders, and others who do their best to make our visits to haunts like hers enjoyable–"just a step above sanitation workers," she observed. She also harbored genuine resentment against our government's stance toward the kind of business she operated. She wrote: "The current environment in the United States for hospitality establishments—alcohol pushers—is hostile, unfriendly and treacherous."

Under Lynne Breaux's management, Tunnicliff's was as much a restaurant as a tavern, and her food was outstanding. I was not surprised, then, when she moved on to become president of the Restaurant Association of Metropolitan Washington from 2001 to 2013. Under her guidance, the staff doubled in size and the membership quadrupled. She has been very effective in convincing legislators of the importance of restaurants to the vitality of the community. Most of all, in my opinion, Ms. Breaux brought the Washington dining scene into prominence, a realization of the fact that, life long, she has fought hard for our right to "eat, drink, and be merry!" She is "Miss Hospitality."

I turn attention now to the miracle worker of Buffalo, New York. Patricia Ann ("Prish") Moran single-handedly brought the old Italian section of that city

back to life. If the men officially in charge of city building had as much vision, know-how, and drive as this
woman, our cities would be world-class. In 2007, Prish
acquired a huge old Victorian structure on the corner
of Grant Street and Lafayette Avenue in that rundown
section of West Buffalo. She paid $112,000 for the old
monster and applied her design skills, converting the
ground floor to a coffeehouse and remodeling the upper floors as habitable apartments. Soon enough, that
part of the city came back to life, with people from all
walks of life and all parts of town becoming regulars.

Prish also acquired Billy Sunday's first tabernacle,
located close by, and converted it into a venue for pro-
grams and presentations of public interest. More recently, she acquired a property at 301 Parkside Avenue
and created there a wonderful little pub—the sign over
the door reads simply "P. Moran." Her visits to British
pubs convinced her to create one, and she did it so suc-
cessfully that, once inside, you get the impression that
it's been there for ages. A small place, holding about
thirty patrons comfortably, her pub serves six white
and four red wines, British and Irish beers, plus several
craft beers from the New England area.

While both the food and the drinks served are still
being adjusted to local tastes, I took particular interest in the food menu she sent me. Of course, "bangers
and mash" is on the menu in this English-style pub,

along with Prish's favorite, Irish rice pudding, a German dried sausage platter, melted triple-cream Brie with caramelized apples, and much more. Her menu brought to mind Leonardo Boff, the Brazilian philosopher who was often invited to speak and, afterward, was treated to dinner in upscale restaurants (where he never felt comfortable). He was a champion of the poor, and guilt plagued him in those places. He wrote a little piece entitled "In Praise of Taverns," in which he expressed his preference:

> In this context, the consolation of taverns comes to mind. I like to go to taverns because I can eat there without feeling bad. There are taverns, cantinas, or toscas, all over the world, including the poor communities where I worked for many years. There a true democracy prevails: the tavern (where people with less buying power go) welcomes everybody. A college professor can be there drinking his brandy alongside a construction worker, a stage actor at the same table with a scoundrel, and even the village drunk, who is downing a cold one. One only has to come in, take a seat, and call loudly "pass me a very cold beer."

P. Moran's is on a corner of Parkside Avenue, which means that Prish has to pay the city twice the usual amount for the outdoor seating she offers—she is on *two* streets! In Spain and Portugal, places like hers would not be charged for outdoor seating because it is understood that they do so much for the life of the city and its economic well-being. Will *we* ever learn that hospitality more than pays for itself?

Prish relishes the time she gets to spend with friends in her pub, and she told me of one of her rewards when she's a part of the company: from time to time, she will notice patrons on their little phones explaining that they won't be able to make an appointment elsewhere—they're having too good a time.

Now it's time to wrap up this discussion of female tipplers with a story from the early twentieth century and on this very subject of tippling females. Edward Bok, long-time editor of the *Ladies Home Journal* and the man who gave us the term "living room" instead of parlor or drawing room, sent queries to a sample of fifty prominent women seeking to discover the extent to which they used any of the popular medicines of the day. These included Parker's Tonic, advertised as "purely vegetable and recommended for inebriates," which contained 42 percent alcohol by volume and which was more potent than Mr. Bok's favorite bourbon. Also included was Hoofland's German Bitters, proclaimed to be entirely vegetable and free from "alcoholic stimulant" although it was 26 percent alcohol, as was Kaufman's Sulphur Bitters, which contained no sulfur. Cohen's Liquid Beef Tonic, offered as treatment for the alcohol habit, was 27 percent alcohol or 54 proof. Lydia Pinkham's Vegetable Compound, the most popular of all, contained between 18 and 20 percent alcohol by volume.

What made Bok's survey especially interesting was the fact that these fifty letters were sent to members of the Women's Christian Temperance Union only, and three-fourths of the women regularly used one or more of the highly laced patent medicines.

# 8

## *Cocktail Parties*

---

One of many differences between the barroom and the cocktail party is that many unkind words are said about barrooms by people who don't drink, whereas many unkind things are said about cocktail parties by people who do drink. I'll give the latter folks due voice beginning with C. Northcote Parkinson, the British naval historian and author who observed that the Chinese word for cocktail party means, literally, "two hours standing up." The imperative is to remain standing and circulate, and after everyone has "chatted" with everyone else, they are free to leave. The novelist Paul Gallico spared little in his denunciation: "I hate cocktail parties. To be invited to one is an insult; to be present is a bore. I must have attended more than a hundred in my lifetime and cannot remember once having a good time."

Lawrence Durrell, whose writing has probably done more for Greek Island tourism than any tourist bureau, counters the argument that the cocktail party is a by-product of Prohibition. No, says he: "The cocktail party—as the name itself indicates—was originally invented by dogs. They are simply bottom-sniffings raised to the rank of formal ceremonies." P. G. Wodehouse, who has found more delight in boy-girl relations and the game of golf than anyone I've ever read, has captured the sheer excitement of the cocktail party: "It's one of those parties where you cough twice before you speak and then decide to say nothing at all."

William Cole, editor and writer of whimsical poetry, offered a telescopic view of cocktail parties, seeing them as "a hundred standing people smiling and talking to one another, nodding like gooney birds." Lucius Beebe caught the essence of a cocktail party as he's experienced it: "Where they give you a canapé and a napkin and it doesn't matter which one you put in your mouth—both taste the same." Perhaps the worst was offered by theater critic Brooks Atkinson: "The cocktail party has the form of friendship without the warmth and devotion. It is the device for getting rid of social obligations hurriedly en masse, or for making overtures toward more serious social relationships, as in the art of whoring."

The anthropologist Weston La Barre once published a satire on cocktail parties in which a mythical African counterpart studied "Koktel Partis" in the United States, where they were invented. He focused on the main season for them—from harvest time to the New Year. Social status, he noted, is indicated by the number of such ordeals to which one is invited. Complaining about too many invitations is a matter of polite boasting. Because of multiple commitments, the "elite" leave these parties early, and they always say that they "hate to go," though it is plain that they would really hate to stay.

But whence the cocktail party? It belongs to the category of disputed origins, a game some people love, for as soon as a claim is made, the rush is on to dispute it. For a while credit was given to British novelist Alec Waugh, brother of Evelyn, who invited friends over in the early evening and, instead of serving the expected tea, poured out Rum Swizzles (the national drink of Bermuda). That was in 1925 (we're pretty sure), but Waugh himself said it was the painter C. R. W. Nevinson who, the year before, introduced the first cocktail party in England. But thanks to the St. Paul Pioneer Press, we learn that a Mrs. Walsh in St. Louis invited fifty people over for drinks in May of 1917 (are you keeping track?). But again, Google tells us that Mrs. Richard S. Dana, way back in September of 1890 gave an eggnog party at her home, and I'll bet you don't care anymore.

The real impetus behind both cocktails *and* parties was Prohibition. During Prohibition, wine was very scarce as the bootleggers mainly trafficked in spirits. Bootleg booze was most often in need of something to "ease" the taste, and that need gave rise to all sorts of cocktail creations. Since one could no longer drink in public restaurants, having dinner parties in private homes became very popular during this time. Many speakeasies served dinners, but they were expensive and might be raided. In some homes, cocktails were served beforehand to those who wished to partake in a room apart from the dining room, and water was served with dinner. In other homes, cocktails substituted for wine at the table. Dinner parties at home continued to be popular after repeal, during the Depression years, as times were hard and doing so was cheaper.

Nowadays, cocktail parties are used for a variety of reasons: to introduce new staff members, to show off a new house, to celebrate anniversaries, to announce a new product or service. Are they always the disagreeable affairs so many of our wits accuse them of being? Assuredly, we can all remember drinking alcoholic beverages in more comfortable settings. Standing with a drink in one's hand for an hour or more is far from ideal, but a blanket indictment is most misleading. I offer an example of some highly successful cocktail parties in the context of a new university, in which parties are very important in getting a multitude of new faculty and staff to get to know one another.

In the autumn, with the opening of the school year and new faculty and staff aboard, cocktail parties were in full swing. They were hierarchical and discriminating; to be invited at the highest level was an "honor." We didn't all fit where we were supposed to. Some balked at the black tie requirement. Some didn't bother to learn the names of and properly address the wives of the president and vice president, to say nothing of the provost and deans.

The wife of the chair of philosophy understood all of this, and she instituted what she dubbed "The Dregs of Society" cocktail party, an instant success. The "outcasts" got along with one another famously, and word got around that Miss Betty's parties were the best—what *fun* they were! By the third year, those not invited to one of Miss Betty's parties could only envy those who were. Her major effort in these affairs was to slow-cook a beef roast in a closed outdoor grill. The beverage duties were assigned to her husband.

Cocktail parties can be successful, and I suspect most of them are. If anyone insists on comparing them to more laid-back and comfortable occasions, appreciate them for what they are and compare them, also, with an interaction that takes place electronically with members of one's "network." Cocktail parties are face-to-face occasions where we engage people who are new, and often interesting, to us. If that fails you, recall what the author H. S. Leigh referred to as "the rapturous, wild, and ineffable pleasure of drinking at someone else's expense."

Finally, on cocktail parties, be advised that there is more to managing a successful one than the novice might imagine. As I've already made clear, I'm averse to giving instructions on any aspect of tippling, but I've checked the internet and found it full of useful advice and forewarnings on the subject.

# 9

# *Toasting and Roasting*

Toasting and roasting are great aids to the enjoyment of drinking—they help to break the ice, they let grown men and women tease, taunt, and openly express affection and gratitude without seeming childish or maudlin. And yet good toasts are akin to acts of heroism: they are infrequent and brief but earn a lasting reputation. The bon mot! The perfectly phrased toast, the proper pronouncement at the proper moment not only marks the occasion and the honoree but the speaker as well.

## *Toasts*

The word *toast* may originate in the seventeenth-century English habit of flavoring wine with spiced toast,

which may have absorbed some of the harsh taste. The things they had to put with in the past! While drinking to one's health seemed like nothing but a very good idea at that time, this gracious and ennobling custom was banned in Massachusetts back in 1634. That colony's esteemed leaders called it an "abominable ceremony," proving once again that England was getting shed of its worst. Thankfully, the people ignored the law completely. In 1645, said law was repealed, lest it seem that the people were more capable than their elected officials.

Many toasts one hears are pro forma but appropriate, and there's no problem with that. Seasonal toasts may be of that nature, but so much time has passed that they seem new and original. I like the prolific writer and historian Hilaire Belloc's holiday toast, which goes as follows:

May all good fellows that here agree
Drink Audit Ale in Heaven with me
And all my enemies go to hell!
Noel! Noel! Noel! Noel!

Feel free to substitute what you will for Audit Ale—Anchor Steam, Guinness, Liebfraumilch, whatever—but I doubt there's any Miller Lite in heaven.

In China, toasting is a delicate matter, and one should never forget one's station in life or at the table, or raise a cup higher than your superior or elder does. Toasts may be orders, such as *ganbei*, which means "dry cup" (and that is what you should have by the time you put your cup down), or something more polite, along the lines of "I'll drink this but you can drink as much as you want." People never drink without initiating a toast or inviting others at the table to drink. This often occurs in a business setting and sets the tone for future dealings.

In the United States, toasts are more informal and even humorous. But tongue-in-cheek toasts are not real toasts but parodies of them, and one should not still a large audience with them. They are for the immediate circle. A few examples include "Here's how we lost the farm!" and what might be called the "bum's toast": "Here's to the holidays—all 365 of them!"

I count it a sacred duty to help the Irish celebrate their day, and every tippler deserving of the name will agree. Here's the routine. Arise by midmorning and have a generous, fortifying breakfast. Insert the movie *The Quiet Man* in your player and watch attentively, drinking nothing. When the movie is over, put on something green, take your wonderful thirst to the place where the kinsmen have gathered, and have the grandest time at it. Do not forget to toast St. Patrick. You may wish to use this one:

> St. Patrick was a gentleman
> Who through strategy and stealth
> Drove all the snakes from Ireland
> Here's a bumper to his health.
> But not too many bumpers,
> Lest we forget ourselves, and then
> Forget the good St. Patrick
> And see the snakes again.

That toast, all eight lines of it, may be more than you will remember. In such case, there is an Irish bull that may be used: "Let us get down on our knees and thank God that we are still on our feet."

Your computer will supply you with far more clever toasts than you'll ever use, so I will close the topic here with two in Latin, as it is sometimes such fun to appear to be well educated. To say "Cheers," it's *Salutaria*. "I drink to your health" is *Propino tibi salutem*, which is still used today in Italy.

## *Roasts*

Solidarity in human relationships is no more evident than in a roast. The "honoree" is made to suffer a nasty, vicious, lying attack before an audience, and he laughs as loud as anyone else in the room. The only justification one needs for saying the absolute worst about the victim is that it be good for a laugh.

Contrary to the impression sometimes given by televised entertainers, the Friars Club did not invent the roast. Not only the roast, but its gate-opening embellishment—the heckle—come to us courtesy of Philadelphia's Clover Club. There were earlier versions in England, but the American origin is the Clover. First meeting early in 1882, the Clover Club took its name from a couplet in an old minstrel song. The couplet itself became the club's motto, and it is one that tipplers might well appreciate: "When we live, we live in clover / When we die, we die all over." It isn't clear just when heckling was introduced into the routine of the club's roasts. It may have been present in the beginning or it may not, but a journalist's report in 1939 testified to its firm place in the order of things by that time. Writing for the *Philadelphia Inquirer*, Alex Kendrick noted that the club's unwritten law is that every man has the right to speak, and every man has the right to heckle.

Obviously, the rule maximizes participation. Anybody may rise to speak, not just those seated at the head table. More importantly, anybody in the room may assail the roasters as well as the honoree, and he may do so at any time. He who rises to lampoon may get as well as he gives. This may be of some consolation to the honoree.

"It doesn't get any better than this!" says an overworked beer commercial depicting "the boys" sitting around the campfire after a day of fishing. Oh yes it does, and those privileged to be present at a roast and heckle know it well. Modest amounts of alcohol are essential to the roast and heckle, as the mood becomes festive after the first drink, and before long those otherwise a little timid about speaking begin popping up all over the place.

The success of roasts depends upon their infrequency. They are special events usually associated with retirement, reunions, relocations, and the like, though far less often with birthdays—maybe a man's fiftieth. Women seem exempted from that kind of thing.

A monthly or even a quarterly roast would soon be the death of one of the finest tipples a group can manage.

Unfortunately, political correctness has crept in, as it has in far too many areas of life these days. The new idea is that if it's fun, everybody should be able to enjoy it, even those for whom the word *camaraderie* vastly overstates the quality of their associations. The "corrected" version of a roast is usually called a "broast," the kinder, gentler production in which a little teasing is acceptable but even that is overwhelmed by all the expressions of fondness for the character upon whom the light shines. It is, make no mistake, unfair to insult anyone at these affairs. Feelings might be hurt!

With the fainthearted in mind, the choice of honorees and guests at roasts should be carefully considered. At one of ours, most of us were having at the victim in grand style when one among us rose to give a heartfelt speech, lauding the man's contributions. The mood was shot, and worse, the honoree went around afterward telling everyone how much he appreciated the kind remarks of the compassionate one. We roasters regretted the time we'd spent in preparation. Our carefully prepared nastiness was upstaged by a big dose of impromptu syrup. Moral: Never roast a weak ego.

Whereas you may find gobs of clever toasts on the internet, the barbs typically aimed at the honoree will most probably elude you. Let's name the honoree

"George" and take note of how he's treated at a typical roast. I should mention that my good friend and fellow roaster Charles Edgley contributed some of these. ("Edge" and I both learned the catechism of symbolic interactionism. He remained true to the faith and contributed significantly. I went astray, but we remained united as friends, and tipplers.)

A few words about "George":

This man needs no introduction—what he needs is a conclusion.

George once ran unopposed in a local election and lost.

George once sent his picture to a Lonely Hearts Club, and they sent it back, saying they weren't that lonely.

I'm not saying George is that old but restaurants make him pay in advance.

When his wife wanted to celebrate their anniversary, he suggested a few moments of silence.

"Do I have the biggest feet in the third grade because I'm Norwegian?" George asked his Dad. "No," his father replied, "It's because you're nineteen."

The doctor told George's wife, "I don't like the way your husband looks." "Neither do I," she said, "but he's good with the kids."

Waiting for George to make it big is like leaving a light on for Jimmy Hoffa.

George has lots of friends in high places—trouble is they all throw coconuts at him.

But no more about George's sex life—what is past, is past.

First of all, let's review George's major accomplishments—there, that didn't take long, did it?

The reader who has suffered through these barbs will well understand why the "roastee" laughs as much as the rest of the gang. The "insults" are patently ridiculous. As comedian Milton Berle once observed, the roast is a "crazy way to tell a man that you love him."

Yet even if you're never lucky enough to roast or be roasted, you'll find a similar sort of fun on display in many taverns and pubs. Impoliteness here is really a means of communicating affection, with humor added to aid in digestion. For example, what to say to express joy at seeing a friend already in place at the bar? How about "If I'd known you were here, I'd have kept on going." This could be followed up with "Don't you ever do any work?" And then to the host or hostess, "Why do you keep letting him in here? What kind of a place are you running?" The victim and the assailant should probably be on very good terms, such that their relationship is not fragile. But this is really an invitation to a duel of wits, and a notice to all present: I'm here to enjoy myself. Join in!

# 10

# *Pests and Killjoys*

Tipplers have no real enemies for the same reason that eagles do not do battle with cowbirds. There are many people out there who'd like to deny us our pleasures, and they try, but we persevere. History is on our side, to say nothing of Manifest Destiny, the example set by all other advanced cultures, and the promise of the Scriptures.

We have no real enemies, but we do live in a meddlesome society where the imperative to "live and let live" no longer holds sway. We don't suffer pestilence, but we do suffer pests. We shall look at them in turn—the drunks, the bores, the puritans, and the government. The first pest and the easiest to dispense with is the drunkard. We virtually never have to confront one.

They exist, of course, but not in the venues where we tipple. We resent them because the enemies of alcohol hold them up as proof and validation of their claims, and use that example in their attempts to deprive the overwhelming majority of responsible drinkers of their enjoyment.

What we tipplers do sometimes confront is the fellow who has had "a little too much to drink." As the old proverb has it, a little too much is much too much, and we fully understand and agree because, aside from the bad manners and disgusting spectacle, the drunk presents tactical problems. Who will look after him? How will he get home? Should he remain on the invitation list?

Bores are a more frequently encountered problem and a formidable one. There are several types of bores, several ways of draining the life out of otherwise scintillating interaction. Some sit there like a lump of clay, some complain about everything, some are masters of banality, and some dominate conversation as though the rest of us are really interested. It is amazing that people like this seem totally unaware of the fact that they are boring people to death.

The major problem with such bores is that we can't avoid them as we'd like. They are part of our social circle and must be too much a part of our socializing. I have no solution to the problem of the bore once she or he is being entertained in our home. I can only protect myself, which is to use any excuse to leave the room and hope that others will follow my lead. My wife and I used to entertain in two rooms, but I added a third, and escape is very easy now.

The bore is no problem at all for that gang of tipplers who meet on a very regular basis at a time and tavern of their choosing. Anyone who talks too much or says things at odds with the rhythmic flow of conversation is simply told to shut his mouth.

The most comical among those pests tipplers have had to contend with are the puritans, whose name derives from their forebears' attempt to purify the Church of England. Would they have stayed there, but in 1630 the good ship *Arbella* deposited them at Salem harbor and those of the down-turned mouth have done their best to keep us unhappy ever since. Their thinking traces back to John Calvin's notion of "natural depravity," which asserts that "the mind of man is so entirely alienated from the righteousness of God that he cannot conceive, desire, or design anything but what is wicked, distorted, foul, impure, and iniquitous."

H. L. Mencken described Puritanism as "the haunting fear that someone, somewhere, may be happy." He said other things about them but in a language I have to avoid. Today's puritans, some of whom are the "religious right," are far more concerned about uniting the church and state, and combating LGBT (lesbian, gay, bisexual, and transgender) rights than their earlier campaign against alcohol. Actually, as they now "allow" careful drinking and oppose drunkenness, we are almost bedfellows; but they'll still close a tavern any chance they get. What made them comical were their earlier attempts to correct God's Word and, as I promised to make this book entertaining, we shall revisit that comedy. *The Temperance Bible Commentary* was published in London and devoted itself to "correcting" God's Word. "Stay me with flagons" in the Song of Solomon was changed to "Sustain me with a cake of grapes," and "A feast of wine in the lees" in Isaiah became "A feast of preserves, well clarified."

In 1872, the English Cardinal Manning issued a warning to them but to no apparent avail: "I repeat distinctly that any man who should say that the use of wine . . . is sinful when it does not lead to drunkenness, that man is a heretic condemned by the Catholic Church." The author and social historian Bernard Rudofsky, among others, took note of this "interesting aspect of American religion"—attempting to be holier than the Lord. He wrote:

> Let us not forget that Christ Himself gave his seal
> of approval to wine and wine drinking. Not to let

the wedding party down, He miraculously transformed water into wine, and one of the last dispositions in his earthly life was to elevate the partaking of bread and wine to a holy sacrament. Only a profoundly impious nation could have committed the blasphemy of outlawing wine.

Two Scotsmen offered a prize for the best essay "proving" that the Bible does not mean what it says. The winning effort came to be known as the "two wine theory" by virtue of which the "Drys" argue that the wine of the Last Supper or that which Christ made from water was unfermented grape juice. Fermentation, however, could not be stopped by the ancient Hebrews even if they had wished to do so. Moreover, the Old Testament uses four different words to distinguish types of fermented wine, and one to identify strong drink. Where wine is mentioned, it is always and necessarily fermented.

Particularly irksome to the fanatics is the twenty-third verse of First Timothy, wherein Paul gives Timothy this advice: "Drink no longer water, but use a little wine for thy stomach's sake and for thine often infirmities." *The Temperance Bible Commentary*, in addressing this passage, contended that Paul meant this advice for Timothy alone and did not presume to act as physician-general to the Christian world for all ages.

Ah, so! To whom do the Scriptures speak, only to those long dead and gone to their reward?

Another manifestation of the diminished mental capacity of such folks is their frequent contention that all of society's problems would disappear if everyone stopped drinking alcoholic beverages. That would mean no more poverty, no more sex offenses, no more robbery, no avarice in business dealings, and so on. Sane people react in different ways to such fatuity. In a state of exasperation, the Irish writer Maurice Healy once demanded that these people answer a "straight question": "On what principle do they justify their attempt to cut off all men from something which, apart from Divine sanction, has been used by all civilized races since the beginning of recorded time?"

The "principle," of course, is blasphemy, and one is given to wonder why self-proclaimed Christians would risk God's wrath by distorting His Word, or why they would so distort their religion as to turn reasonable persons away. Tipplers, as one might guess, prefer the humorous response, particularly those that reverse the message, as was cleverly done by author and columnist Don Marquis speaking as "The Old Soak." Here is his "testimonial":

> Years ago I used to struggle, and think maybe I would quit drinking sometime, and it kept me

unhappy. But as soon as I come right out and acknowledged that booze was my Boss and Master, and set him up and crowned him King, a great peace fell unto me, and I ceased to struggle, and I have been happy and contented and full of love for my fellow man ever since.

When the Reverend Dr. John Roach Stanton of the Calvary Baptist Church invited Mencken to his church, "where I shall administer a theological spanking," Mencken declined the invitation, explaining that he didn't go to cabarets or low places of any kind and that he was trying to live a moral life there in Baltimore. As to the Reverend Doctor's praying for him, Mencken regretted that the effect was much more feeble than it used to be—formerly it made his head spin, but more recently it just made his throat dry.

When last in the area, I purchased a Roanoke, Virginia, newspaper and, with little to do at the time, read it rather thoroughly and came across the following from a local Baptist:

When you go to church you will leave renewed, uplifted and in a better frame of mind than when you went in. When you leave a bar or tavern, except for the alcohol you consumed or the disease you came into contact with or the drugs you picked up, you will leave as empty as when you went in.

One must assume that this good Baptist is speculating as to what goes on in a bar, for surely he would never actually enter such a place. When sociologist Marshall Clinard did look into taverns in the state of Wisconsin, he found the majority of people who frequented them considered them to be "social clubs" and "places to meet friends." They considered the tavern especially important because in it they "were free to act and think as they wish," whereas in church and most other gathering places, they were only spectators. We may conclude one of two things regarding that Baptist's take on taverns: either Mencken was correct in his impressions of the South, or our Baptist friend is yet another product of that puritanism that took such a strong hold on the Baptists and Methodists in this nation.

Let us close on the puritans, leaving them a few more Bible offerings to "work on":

He causeth the grass to grow for the cattle, and herb for the service of man: that he may bring forth food out of the earth and wine that maketh glad the heart of man. (Psalm 104)

Give strong drink unto him that is ready to perish, and wine unto those that be of heavy hearts. (Proverbs 31:6)

Let him drink, and forget his poverty, and remember his misery no more. (Proverbs 31:7)

The Bible "improvers" would, I think, have a major problem with the wedding at Cana described in John 2:1–11. To wit:

On the third day there was a wedding in Cana of Galilee, and the mother of Jesus was there. Jesus and his disciples had also been invited to the wedding. When the wine gave out, the mother of Jesus said to him, "They have no wine." And Jesus said to her, "Woman, what concern is that to you and me? My hour has not yet come." His mother said to the servants, "Do whatever he tells you." Now standing there were six stone water jars for the Jewish rites of purification, each holding twenty or thirty gallons. Jesus said to them, "Fill the jars with water." And they filled them up to the brim. He said to them, "Now draw some out, and take it to the chief steward." So they took it. When the steward tasted the water that had become wine, and did not know where it came from (though the servants who had drawn the water knew), the steward called the bridegroom and said to him, "Everyone serves the good wine first, and then the inferior wine after the guests have become drunk. But you have kept the good wine until now." Jesus did this, the first of his signs, in Cana of Galilee, and revealed his glory, and his disciples believed in him.

We close this little discussion of puritan antics with a favorite quotation from Martin Luther, beautiful in its simplicity: "He who loves not wine, women and song remains a fool his whole life long."

The biggest and baddest of pests is the government, and we deserve much better than we get. In his classic volume on Scotch, the journalist and author Sir Robert Lockhart registered amazement that we Yanks, who combine rugged individualism with high idealism, would have accepted Prohibition. In fact, we the people did not accept it. Many of our cities, New York included, had more illegal speakeasies after passage than they had legal saloons before. Many who had never drunk before protested by taking up the habit. Female drinking increased because the "speaks" admitted the women barred from saloons earlier on. I once asked my father how one could get a drink when in a strange city. "Ask the nearest cop," he said.

We the people did not accept what Mencken called an "infamous and tyrannical" assault upon our liberties. It was imposed by inept politicians posing as statesmen. The Temperance Movement actually started as an educational endeavor on the part of reasonable men and women. Soon, however, the fanatics took over, and they were not to be satisfied with educating, nor with limiting sales to beer and wine, nor even leaving it to state law, wherein the voters could decide whether to "go dry" or not. No, the fanatics pushed for nothing less than amendment to the Constitution.

Statesmen, had there been a sufficient number of them in the House and Senate, would have served as a check on this lunacy. Our elected officials, however, fell right in line. Their ilk would like us to forget Prohibition, but the fact is that distrust of government did not begin with Vietnam or Watergate. It was Prohibition that taught the American people to distrust the law of the land. It was Prohibition that corrupted police departments the country over, and it was Prohibition that gave us organized crime.

Enforcement was enacted via the National Prohibition Act of 1919, nicknamed the Volstead Act. Violation was a misdemeanor with a maximum fine of $1,000 and a maximum of six months in prison for the first offense. Confronted with overwhelming failure of enforcement, Congress passed the Jones Act the following year, which made violation a felony with a maximum fine of $10,000 and five years in prison for the first offense. It was known as the "five and ten" law.

The new penalties were so blatantly excessive that many former Drys joined the Wets. Judges all over the nation also balked. In 1931, the year before repeal, actual fines averaged between $100 and $250, prompting the US attorney general to accuse judges of "cheapening justice." A pattern of enacting in ignorance and enforcing with arrogance is all too typical of our federal government, as much now as it was back then. Recent evidence is found in the bullying tactics of the Bureau of Alcohol, Tobacco, Firearms and Explosives (ATF) following a *60 Minutes* report on the French paradox—the gist of which is that moderate consumption of red wine is good for one's health. The ATF threatened several small wineries with loss of their licenses if they did not stop publication of reprints of that report.

The ranks of federal agencies concerned with alcohol production and consumption are filled with Drys and are anti-alcohol. They impose huge taxes on the industry and use those funds to do it in. It is only equitable that people have lost respect for politicians—they have none for us.

As for state governments, talk to anyone operating or attempting to operate a tavern. In California, which is typical, legendary bar owner Sean Mooney encountered state law in the form of "270 pages of impenetrable prose" that is subject to change at every meeting of the legislature. Mooney found it "full of traps and pitfalls." Were it not for the government's fondness for tax money, it is doubtful we'd have any bars at all. It should be noted that eighteen of the fifty states have abolished the American idea of free enterprise in the area of alcohol sales. These states have assumed monopoly control over the sale of alcoholic beverages.

Municipal governments get credit for accomplishing what the Anti-Saloon League of Prohibition days could not—the virtual elimination of the tavern. While they still exist, we've lost more than two-thirds the number we had at the end of World War II. What's done most of them in is negative zoning that prohibits not only taverns but any kind of commercial enterprise where people might otherwise gather in our residential areas. Thus protected from community, we live highly privatized lives and have become a highly fragmented, politically impotent population. Government likes it that way.

The colossal failures of government would humble decent men and women, but in our case they serve only as arguments for more spending and more regulations. Summing up the aftermath of Prohibition, the historian Herbert Asbury wrote:

The Drys lied to make Prohibition look good; the Wets lied to make it look bad; the government officials lied to make themselves look good and to frighten Congress into giving them more money to spend; and the politicians lied through force of habit.

By the bye, do you know why Prohibition ended? I googled it one day and read the following: "The 18th Amendment was repealed because too many Americans did not support Prohibition." Not quite, dear reader. It was not a concession to what we the people wanted; it was *money*. Following the Great Depression, government desperately needed the money that the taxes on alcoholic beverages had supplied; further, enforcement was expensive and ineffective, and the government couldn't afford it. If you believe our government has learned from its mistakes, take a close look at the War on Drugs, and the costs and consequences thereof.

Prohibition is gone but the mentality that produced it is still very much evident in these United States, nor is it aimed only at those of us who enjoy alcoholic beverages. The inscription on the first coin minted in America was "Mind Your Business." Has it always been the habit of Americans to meddle in other people's affairs? Perhaps, but only in the past two or three generations has it become a national obsession. The words that come out of our mouths, and the food and drink that goes in, rank highly among the myriad faults we find in one another and choose not to ignore. In response to this unbecoming blemish on our national character, I commend and recommend a book by two colleagues, Charles Edgley and the late Dennis Brissett, titled *A Nation of Meddlers*. Can we begin to temper our criticism with a little compassion for fellow citizens? But now that we have dispensed with our pests and killjoys, for the moment, let's move on to more practical matters such as what, when, and how to drink.

# 11

# *The Wine Racket*

"No nation is drunk where wine is cheap."
—Thomas Jefferson

The British journalist Andrew Barr, author of the definitive work entitled *Drink: A Social History of America* (1999), observed that all wine in (our) restaurants is absurdly expensive. I call it a racket, not that the rip-offs are illegal but in agreement with the fourth definition of *racket* in my *Webster's*, to wit, "an easy and profitable means of livelihood." Among many disturbing things about the use of alcohol in our society, I find this one especially galling. Wine should be taken at meals both to enhance the experience and to slow it down, but far too many of us find restaurant wine too expensive to enjoy.

In the locality of my youth, people got by with beer and booze save for a household here and there where a bottle of Manischewitz appeared during the holidays. I first drank wine while living in France from 1955 to 1956. Water from the tap wasn't clear, and little things could be seen floating in it, so we "went native" and drank wine at home. It was red and had no name; it was bulk wine with a pleasant taste. One took an empty bottle to the local grocer who filled it for the equivalent of eight cents American. We weren't getting a break on the price, as the French were all but stingy in these matters. When asking for sugar at a local café, we Americans were surprised at how small their cubes were and, as one journalist put it, the ham in their *jambon* sandwich was "so thin one could read *La Monde* right through it." Eight cents for twenty-five ounces of wine! I could never have suspected that we'd be paying two or three dollars an ounce for this beverage in restaurants one day.

The first thing to understand, as one attempts to account for the ridiculously high cost of wine at the consumer level, is that your government not only wants it that way but, upon repeal of the Eighteenth Amendment, enacted legislation to ensure it. The inefficient and costly "three-tier" system of distribution, wherein cost is added each step of the way, was deliberately created to lower the consumption of wine. Things have changed. Massachusetts had been violating the interstate commerce clause of the US Constitution for some time. It required liquor stores and restaurants to buy from wholesalers. It was a real racket. However, that all changed a few years back: the state legislature, much to the chagrin of the wholesalers, passed a law saying restaurants, liquor stores, and individuals could buy from anyone. Sadly, very few restaurants or liquor stores have taken advantage of the change; they like the convenience of buying from the wholesalers in spite of their mediocre offerings.

The three tiers are vineyard, distributor, and retailer, and today some of the largest wine sellers, known as "urban vintners," own few or no vineyards. The retailers divide into two kinds, the bottle shops and the restaurants. Government regulations favor the distributors who, unlike the vineyards and the retailers need not fear economic recessions. Recessions wreak havoc on both the vineyards and the retailers, but the distributors always run in the black because what they pay their people is tied to sales. The State-Mandated Three-Tiered System (SMTTS) has made it possible for a small cartel of distributors to effectively control the industry with their own interests uppermost. From the producers' point of view, repeal of SMTTS is essential to their well-being and is past due.

The major markups in wine are committed in the restaurants. There are "industry standards" that probably have some influence, and, not surprisingly, those "standards" favor the restaurant. For example, a single bottle of wine can be sold a glass at a time and contain four, five, or six ounces per glass. As the cost of the first glass reimburses the cost of that wine to the house, the profit per bottle can easily be 300 percent, 400 percent, or 500 percent. The industry standard gives the house 500 percent. On the sale of a whole bottle, the standard is more generous to the consumer. A bottle of wine selling at $20 in the bottle shop should garner the house $60 or $80, with a maximum of 400 percent profit.

In many restaurants, those who order wine by the glass are not "preferred customers" and are treated accordingly. Mike Shor, the economist who studied thirty-eight of Nashville's wine-selling restaurants, offered the following advice for those wanting only a glass of wine: "Order mid-list. The second-least-expensive wine on the list is often marked up the most. Why? People don't want to look cheap, so they order the second cheapest wine." Shor says, "Go one or two bottles higher for a better deal."

We select one wine over others because of how it tastes, but there are thousands of wines, and each year the taste may change, so we must not only choose among types of wine and the vineyard but also the vintages. It's too much! So we have expert wine tasters to guide us in our selections. How does that work out?

In 2001, Frederick Brochet, a PhD candidate in France, gave twenty-seven females and twenty-seven males glasses of both white and red wines and asked them to describe the taste of each. For the white wine, the most often used descriptors were "floral," "honey," "peach," and "lemon." For the reds, the adjectives most commonly used were "raspberry," "cherry," "cedar," and "chicory." A week later he gave them another two glasses of wine, a white and another white with a taste-less red dye in it and asked them to describe the taste of each. The fake red elicited most of the same descriptors as the real ones had had.

But those tasters were students. How accurate are the professional wine tasters? In 2005, Robert Hodgson, a retired oceanographer and wine enthusiast, convinced the chief judge of America's oldest and most prestigious wine-tasting organization to allow him an experiment with the judges. Interspersed with the wines being tasted were three of the same wines from the same bottle. The result: "Even trained, professional palates are terrible at judging wine." A wine tasted and rated "good" would get an "excellent" rating a few minutes later. About 10 percent of the judges did a fair job, but their seeming superiority disappeared the following year. As wine prices have been based on these tests, Hodgson's findings were upsetting to say the least.

An even more damning study was reported a few years back. The American Association of Wine Economists analyzed the results of thirteen US wine competitions in which 2,440 wines were entered in three or more competitions around the country. A whopping 47 percent of them won gold medals, but 84 percent of those, when entered in other competitions, received no medals—not even a bronze.

One taster and wine critic, by accurately predicting the high quality of a 1982 Bordeaux wine, became famous and proceeded to popularize a 100-point wine-rating system. Each tested wine started with 50 points, to which up to 5 more would be added for "color and appearance," up to 15 points more for "aroma and bouquet," another 20 for "flavor and finish," and up to 10 points for its "potential." The scale became extremely popular.

When interviewed for the *Atlantic Monthly*, critic Robert Parker told the author that he tastes ten-thousand wines a year and "remembers every wine he has tasted over the past thirty-two years and, within a few points, every score he has given as well." Yet in a public blind tasting of fifteen top wines from Bordeaux 2005, which he called "the greatest vintage of my lifetime," he could not correctly identify any of them, and he confused the Right Bank with the Left Bank regions several times.

When Princeton's brilliant economist Orley Ashenfelter introduced science to the matter of predicting the quality of Bordeaux wines, Parker was quick to call these efforts an absurd and ludicrous scam. To oversimplify, Ashenfelter held soil and vineyards constant in his study and tracked the weather, discovering that wet winters followed by hot and dry summers produced the best wines barring heavy rainfalls at harvest time. This method seems to work.

If tasting is so unreliable and Parker comes off as a bit of a con man, why does his rating system remain so popular? Because it sells wine!

So given the failings of the experts, what criteria are we left with? You guessed it—the price we have to pay for the wine.

Now, in using price as a guide to wine selection, it should first be realized that there are two approaches: one that includes all wines for consideration, and one that insists anything under $20 is not worth consideration. When it comes to discerning wines, snobbery and ignorance will always be with us. For what it is worth in facing the task of finding the right items in your store, I offer the results obtained by the novelist and journalist Will Starr and his friends who have tried "a lot of wines from the bottom up." Yet even they didn't start at the bottom, with "Two Buck Chuck" and Oak Leaf, which have a lot of fans and are well under $5:

$5 "Not very good"
$10 "Gets better"
$15 "Pretty damn good"
$20 "From there to $200, it doesn't get any better"

Now it's time to confess. Of all the kinds of alcoholic drinks one can purchase in bars or restaurants, including tap beer, brand bottled beer, craft beer, brand liquor, bottom-shelf liquor, and wine, wine has the lowest markup. So why do I pick on wine? Because it makes the meal and 300 percent profit on an essential is profoundly irritating. But for distributors' profits and the fact that the government gets more tax money from costlier products, we could and should be paying considerably less.

Price, after all, isn't everything. The Lenox Wine Club in Massachusetts, according to host Elliott Morss, found that supermarket boxed wines often won its blind tastings. When it comes to wine, as it is with beef steaks, cigars, Scotch whiskies, and

cheeses, to name some of the more obvious desid-
erata that give us pleasure, taste is everything. Morss
tells us, "I drink box wines at home from a small
decanter. When we go to dinner parties, I also take
box wines as house gifts. They make for interesting
discussions!"

# 12

## *Beer: The Staff of Life*

By a small margin, beer remains America's favorite alcoholic beverage, with wine in second place and hard liquor lagging far behind them both. We now have over four thousand breweries in the United States, and three-fourths of the adult population live within ten miles of a brewery. With all this beer around us, I think it's time to ask a most relevant question: what exactly is beer?

Distillation seems a rather straightforward chemical process, but fermentation is mysterious indeed. One is led to believe that "little things," when added to the right solutions, get active and do their "little things" and voilà!—beer is the result. That was the extent of my grasp until Ted Bass, head brewer at Santa Rosa Bay Brewing Company in Fort Walton, Florida,

shared a copy of the true explanation that he, in turn, was provided while a student in a brewer's program. The secret was revealed way back in 1839 in volume 29 of the German journal that translates as *Annals of Chemistry*, in a submission by the internationally renowned chemists Friedrich Wöhler and Justus von Liebig. Here is the translation:

Beer yeast, when dispersed in water, breaks down into an infinite number of small spheres. If these spheres are transferred to an aqueous solution of sugar they develop into small animals. They are endowed with a sort of suction trunk with which they gulp up the sugar from the solution. Digestion is immediately clearly recognizable because of the discharge of excrements. These animals evacuate ethyl alcohol from their bowels and carbon dioxide from their urinary organs. Thus one can observe how a specifically lighter fluid is exuded from the anus and rises vertically whereas a stream of carbon dioxide is ejected from their enormously large genitals.

It's always been my experience that foods and beverages are rendered all the more enjoyable when the matter of how they are produced and prepared is known. In this respect I am most happy to have contributed to the reader's enjoyment of beer.

The word *beer* derives from the Latin *bibere*, which means "to drink." In German it's *bier*, in French *bière*, and in Italian *birra*. Its popularity began in northern Europe, where the grapevines don't grow. While Germany improved the quality of beer and its taverns became legendary for the pleasant and friendly feelings (the gemütlichkeit) that pervaded them, the exhilarating drink did not catch on in Italy where, according to Bob Brown (*Let There be Beer!*), the Emperor Julian had argued that beer is only the bastard son of malt, whereas wine is the legitimate child of Zeus.

Beer's advantage in producing happy times was evident in its low alcohol content. The reveler can drink eight times as much beer as wine to achieve the same degree of bliss; in other words, he can drink all afternoon and evening. As many of you know, there are basically two styles or kinds of beer: ale and lager. Ale has been around for at least five thousand years according to physical evidence, and probably much longer. Lager is only a few hundred years old. The yeast used in making ale (*Saccharomyces cerevisiae*) floats on top in a warm process known as "top fermentation," and it works fairly quickly. The yeast used in brewing lager (*Saccharomyces pastorianus*) sinks to the bottom, takes longer, and requires refrigeration. Before the 1800s, most beer was ale, but today the most popular beer worldwide is pale lager. The contention, sometimes heard, that ale is "satisfying" while lager is "refreshing" is lost on most of us who often drink beer not knowing whether it's ale or lager.

There are other beers, mainly the hybrids, that usually result from a mixing of the techniques used to produce ale and lager. Steam beer, for example, is a lager brewed at higher temperatures and comes out highly effervescent. Altbier is top fermented but stored cold like lagers, ditto for Kölsch and cream ales.

Just as many of us have a favorite table wine, so too we have a "home beer," the brand kept on hand in the fridge. After taking up residence in Florida, I was still buying different brands of beer without a favorite until one day I was reading a book by a British gentleman who stated that Franklin's Family Ale was his "home drink" and had been for years. He proclaimed it to be "an ideal steady drink for all times of day" and went so far as to confess that it was Franklin's affordability that originally attracted him to it.

I took a hard look at what was on the shelves and decided to try Schaefer's with much the same motivation. Schaefer's wasn't exactly cheap, yet it was inexpensive and the slogan nailed it: "Schaefer's is the one beer to have when you're having more than one." My dear friend Eugene Wall, retired helicopter pilot extraordinaire, also liked Schaefer's, and so I created a place for us to enjoy it together. About the same time that I adopted Schaefer's, I built a workshop in my backyard and added a four-foot-wide raised deck in the front. On that deck I mounted a small circular table with outdoor arm chairs on either side. There, at an elevation of not much more than a foot above ground, Gene and I would sit and drink Schaefer's, recounting better days but not better beers.

Alas, Schaefer's is no longer available in our locale. I found its replacement in the store closest to our house, and it was Spaten Optimator, a German doppelbock, a strong lager with 7.6 percent alcohol by volume and enough malt to qualify as one of those "meal in a glass" beers. It costs more, of course, but I didn't drink as much. This was the best beer I'd ever enjoyed, but, alas, it too disappeared. I tried to find out what happened, but my store is one of those where they sell what comes in and can't order anything. Unable to find a suitable replacement for Spaten Optimator, I don't have a home brew anymore, and I'm pretty much off beer.

Since you are well over feeling sorry for me, let's look at the beer that we get from the taps. You might first look at the bartender as she draws your beer (women tend to be the best bartenders). If she first wets that sparkling glass in cold water, then holds it at a slight angle just below the tap and pulls the lever all the way down to fill the glass, she's done it right! The house also wants that beer to taste as good as it can, because it's a high volume moneymaker with the average tavern turning a profit of $400 per keg.

A keg of beer contains 15.5 gallons, or 1,984 ounces. How many glasses of draught does that amount to? Of course, that depends mainly on the size of the glass. There are seven different glass shapes commonly used in the United States, and all of them come in a variety of sizes. Here they are: sham pilsner (8, 9, 10, and

12 ounces), tulip goblet (8, 10, 11, and 12 ounces), footed pilsner (8, 9, and 10 ounces), shell (7, 8, 9, and 10 ounces), hourglass (10, 11, 12, and 13 ounces), mug stein (10, 12, 14, and 16 ounces), and the heavy goblet (9, 10, 12, and 14 ounces).

The amount served to you when you buy a glass of beer is not something strictly regulated in this country. There is no line on the glass to indicate 12 ounces or 16 ounces. Further, it is considered unseemly to ask your server how many ounces of beer you are being served. Most "pints" are probably in the 12- to 14-ounce range. In the average bar, a "pint" probably contains 14 ounces with a 3/4-inch head. When it comes to craft beers, expect the glasses to be different and, with them, the profit margin for the house is a little less.

Also found in Bob Brown's book is an account of his experience with the German "Beer Cure," which he reveals with a colorful introduction:

If you have taken the Grape Cure, the Yeast Cure, the Rest Cure, and the Faith Cure, without result, if
you have tried Hollywood dieting, psychoanalysis, grape nuts, Christian Science and spinach, and been
found wanting, if you have mournfully mooed your

way through the Milk Cure, nibbled bales of bran and

inhaled geysers of medicinal waters without getting

better, it is high time you took the Beer Cure.

Brown was not the first to inform us of Germany's remarkable health secret. That distinction belongs to James G. Huneker, who, in the autumn of 1920, wrote H. L. Mencken and his physician Dr. T. C. Williams, informing them that certain generous quantities of pilsner at only 2 1/2 percent alcohol had cured him of serious ailments while abroad.

But it was Brown who, in 1932, described the beer cure so that all America might receive its benefits. Unfortunately, Brown's work has long since been out of print, and the American medical establishment has seen fit to suppress all knowledge of the beer cure. You may search any of our medical journals until you are blue in the face, and you will not find it!

Owing to the recent success of our politicians in transforming the national outlook from one of healthy skepticism to debilitating cynicism, many readers have probably leapt ahead of me, concluding that all the beer cure amounts to is "drinking a lot of beer." Certainly, that is solid advice, but it falls far short of the real prescription.

Odd that I should have written "prescription" just then, for the word conjures up one of Deutschland's oldest proverbs: "Die Brauerei ist die beste Apotheke" (The brewery is the best pharmacy). Our pharmacists, need I say it, also keep mum about the beer cure.

Brown spent twenty-one pages describing the cure, a quantity I can't spare, and so I will omit the lessons on internal medicines and confine our discussion to the when, where, and how. But first, do *you* need the beer cure? To find out, simply have a glass of beer. If you can't drink it, you are obviously in bad shape and in serious need of the cure. If you enjoyed it, you will enjoy the cure all the more.

But, I hear you cry, if the beer went down OK why should I need the cure? Centuries, my friend, centuries before we Americans got keen on preventative medicine, it was an essential part of the beer cure. Smart motorists change oil before the car really needs it. Crafty women, and men, rub in the aloe before the wrinkles appear. And the example of the tippler himself makes the point. The tippler never *needs* a drink—he just doesn't go that long without one.

If you wisely decide to take the beer cure, Germany is the best place for it. The cost of the trip is offset by the economy of the cure itself. Beer, even in the quantities required, is the great bargain among cures. Germany is recommended not for the quality of the basic ingredient so much as considerations of convenience and attitude, primarily the latter. In Germany, for example, they have "beer nurses." Tending to your needs like the angels of mercy they are, they keep a chart of your dosages so that, at any point in the treatment, you may know exactly how much cure you've had. True, in the United States, we have their counterparts, called "cocktail waitresses," who keep a "tab" for us. But it's the whole difference between tender loving care and slinging suds.

Then there is the matter of the *Kur* (spa, health resort, watering hole, etc.) in which Germany excels. They have huge ones with high ceilings and good air, while ours tend to be small, close, and dark by comparison. Better yet, the patient in Germany will spend most of his time "beer-gardening."

The reports from those who've gone over for the cure in those gardens are nothing short of miraculous. The first stein, they say, seems fairly heavy, the second one lighter, the third even lighter. The patients can feel themselves gaining in health and strength as the treatment continues.

Finally, the Germans encourage *Kur* crawling, with patients walking from one beer garden to another between dosages to enjoy the healing potions in many flavors. We Americans had developed the crawl to an admirable extent until Prohibition was enacted by the Evil Ones, and the practice never recovered.

If you go to Germany, how long should you plan to stay; or, if you take the cure here at home, how long does treatment last? It is no coincidence that the prescribed duration of the cure corresponds exactly to the length of their Oktoberfest. Germans tend toward industriousness and a highly controlled life. Oktoberfest ensures that almost everybody gets the beer cure at least once a year. Two weeks then is perfect—not too short, never too long.

Each day of the cure begins with breakfast in bed, whenever one awakens. Said breakfast should include several rolls, alpine honey, marmalade, fresh butter, and as many soft-boiled eggs as one desires. Strong Viennese coffee with thick dollops of cream is recommended. Most importantly, the patient is to drink one glass of a light beer after breakfast; this is to kindle that thirst to be satisfied later in the day.

As the beer cure is more effective when taken amid pleasant company, do not go out to the *Kuren* until early or midafternoon. Between then and, say, six thirty, drink two quarts of beer, starting with light and progressing to the stronger brews. At six thirty, a light snack is suggested, consisting, perhaps of half a boiled goose, dill pickles, kummel-seed bread, and at least three kinds of cheese. Two quarts of strong beer should be consumed with this snack. Now the patient may go beer-gardening, taking roughly a quart at each stop. This is not something that requires close monitoring. A quart will build the average patient's strength to the point where he can walk miles for the next special treat. He will feel that strength. If the strength for the next walk is not felt, if the patient feels a listlessness or weakness, he should not tire himself. Stay where you are and continue the cure right there. Tomorrow you will be stronger.

How much beer should be consumed during the average day of the cure? At first, fourteen quarts will be too many for most, and four quarts too few; eight quarts is about optimal. The body can process about a quart per hour, which gets the patient home at a reasonable hour so that he can be up by noon of the following day. There is a little "deprivation ploy" that many patients pull on themselves, which, they claim, makes the cure more enjoyable. Some drink nothing but water one of the days and, thereby, build a thirst of incredible proportions such that the remainder of the cure is like being in heaven.

At cure's end, look in the mirror and see the evidence of another German proverb: "Bier und Brot macht die Wangen Rot" (Beer and bread make the face red). Finally, how does the patient retain what he has gained? The advice is simplicity itself and perhaps should be sewn in needlepoint and hung in the living room: "A gallon of beer a day keeps the doctor away."

Speaking of beer gardens, by the bye: we used to have them, imported with immigrants from the Old

Country. In New York, the Atlantic Garden, opened in 1858, was a place where everyone was welcome and social class all but forgotten. As the journalist Junius Browne reported:

> The Atlantic is the most cosmopolitan place of entertainment in the City; for, though the greater part of its patrons are Germans, every other nationality is represented there. French, Irish, Spaniards, Italians, Portuguese, even Chinamen and Indians, may be seen through the violet atmosphere of the famous Atlantic.

What the Atlantic had and every beer garden should have, is gemütlichkeit, a cheerful word for all that is warm, cozy, and neighborly. Inclusiveness is key to this feeling, the sense of being all together—and OK with it. Despite this, the beer gardens of nineteenth-century New York were missing a crucial element of the German originals, as attested by Browne:

> The drinking of the Germans . . . is free from the vices of Americans. The Germans indulge in their lager rationally, even when they seem to carry indulgence to excess. They do not squander their means; they do not waste their time. . . . They take lager as we do oxygen into our lungs—appearing to live and thrive upon it. Beer is one of the social virtues;

Gambrinus a patron saint of every family—the protecting deity of every well-regulated household. The Germans combine domesticity with their dissipation—it is that to them literally—taking with them to the saloon or garden their wives and sisters and sweethearts, often their children, who are a check to any excesses or impropriety, and with whom they depart at a seemly hour, overflowing with beer and *bonhomie*, possessed of those two indispensables of peace—an easy mind and a perfect digestion.

For those who have not dropped this book and arranged a flight to Germany or fallen into unbearable nostalgia for a past we never knew, I close with bits of advice about beer. This is embarrassing for me, as I know that most of my readers already know these things, which is why I put it last. Please consider our protégés in tippling, who may benefit from it, and accept my apologies.

- Beer has three major enemies: heat, light, and travel. Fortunately, heat and light are the worst, and you have control over them. Never store beer where sunlight can reach the containers.
- Beer is about 92 percent water and, contrary to all the advertising about mountain streams, virgin brooks, and spring mountain water, almost any highly purified water will do.

- Do not store beer as long as the manufacturers claim them to be safe to do so. Your limit for canned beer should be two months, not three, and your limit for bottled beer should be three months, not five. Keg beer should be tapped and consumed as soon as possible after purchase.
- The first time a new friend invites you over, ask for a beer. If he has none, find a new friend.
- Any man or woman who professes not to like beer is either incomplete or an artificial person. You may consort with them, but not on any serious level.
- Avoid bars where all the beer is served in frozen glasses, for the beer will be all but tasteless. For the best taste, buy warm beer at the store and refrigerate it before use. Beer that gets too cold or is stored too long loses flavor.
- Learn the basics. Beer is fermented at low temperatures, which leaves the yeast at the bottom. It is, thus, "bottom fermented." Ale is fermented at higher temperatures such that the yeast rises to the top, and is "top fermented." Most bottom-fermented beers are called lagers, and the tradition is German; most ales are top fermented, and the tradition is British. Porter and stout are variations of ale, and both of them are sweeter versions.
- Excellent beer glasses are the "British pint dimple glass mugs," which hold it all and handle nicely.

# 13

## *Pairing Food with Drinks*

---

"I cook with wine, sometimes I even add
it to the food."
—W. C. Fields

Don't drink on an empty stomach. That's one of the first lessons one must learn about drinking alcoholic beverages. Food in the stomach absorbs the alcohol and slows its entrance into the bloodstream, where, once it enters, it's off like a shot to work its effects until oxidized.

Morris Chafetz, one of the first medical doctors to recognize the positive importance of alcohol in our lives (and to write numerous books about it), waxed poetic about that blessed synergism between alcoholic beverages and good food in *Liquor: The Servant of Man*:

> How essential a part of the feast is the drink. What a beautiful procession drink makes with dining, the liquor often so much better and more digestible than the food. How dull the dinner and the party would be without liquor. And how the tongues are loosened, the hearts warmed, the better qualities brought out enabling strangers to overcome shyness. And if the liquor is good, how well we all feel after it the next day, for good liquor and a good drinking experience are the best possible tonics. What incense is to a religious function, drink is to the festive occasion. It enables us to enjoy to the full, with all our senses and emotions, the good things which surround us.

Sooner rather than later, any discussion of alcohol and food will be overtaken by the imperative to pair foods with their wine counterparts. Chafetz would no doubt shake his head at the idea. He did acknowledge an affinity between heavy meats and red wine, and he agreed that bland fish meals could benefit from the acidity of a white wine, but that was the extent of his concession. Beyond that, he felt, it's all superstition. Well, here we have an interesting case wherein superstition has become an industry. The fact now is this: if you are anybody worth knowing, you are able to match the entrée you are serving with its perfect wine companion. I know of no other literature in which the word *perfect* appears as often. It isn't that a given wine simply "goes well" with an entrée; most often it's the "perfect pairing" or the "perfect match."

If a significant portion of the population hearkens to claims about pairing, there's real money to be made. Those who entertain in their homes will stock more wines. People will be tempted to try some of the "perfect pairs" at their dinner tables. Cookbook authors can re-introduce their recipes with a wine suggestion following each one. More wines will be discovered (and sold).

My initial take on wine-food pairing was that it was a harmless pursuit that probably appealed to people with more money than they need, in a culture in which boredom is pandemic: no harm done. Further, wine-pairing enhanced my self-esteem because I have discovered a wine that goes "perfectly" with anything I eat. I may reveal what it is on my deathbed—depends on how I feel.

On further reflection, I realized that wine-pairing, for those who believe in it, is yet another source of stress. Am I failing as a host because I didn't get the pairing right? How many wines should we keep in the house? Am I drinking a wine I really don't like just because it's the correct one? Or, am I avoiding the wine I like because the pairing is not advised?

To the Chinese, drinking has always been an important element of meals and banquets, especially in a business setting. I've heard that the first course of a meal, featuring light dishes, is meant to facilitate the consumption of alcohol, while the other courses consist of heavier meats and rice, which work nicely to slow down the effects of said drinks and keep the atmosphere harmonious and amicable.

In England in the early 1970s, before pairing became a fad, Kingsley Amis devoted two pages of *On Drink* to matching foods with drinks. That chapter is entitled "What to Drink with What," and there's no mention of the word *pairing*. His tongue is often in his cheek here, as he advises the "inexpensive clarets" with English cheeses, or Neuchâtel with fondue "to help force it down." Amis closes his listings with an alcoholic beverage that goes with "anything, everything, or nothing"—can you guess what it is? (Starts with a *c* and ends with an *e*).

Predictably, beer is also being paired not just with cheese but with a whole range of foods. Even spirits are now being paired with a variety of dishes. Did you know that shrimp "cries out" for gin? Actually, during

Prohibition a lot of strong spirits were put on dinner tables as wine was scarce, but repeal put an end to that, until now. The internet, casually perused, will give abundant evidence of just how silly this whole matter of pairing has become. You can find the perfect booze to imbibe while snacking on pretzels, and another for Lucky Charms, and which to pair with Hershey's Kisses, and so on.

During four-hour lunches at the Bay Cafe in Fort Walton, Florida, I was introduced to serious bread-dipping. Bill Campbell, who organized those gatherings, would put out a small bowl to which he added extra-virgin olive oil and something else, probably balsamic vinegar, and we would tear off little pieces of French bread, dip them in the oil, and eat them. It went well with the wines we were drinking, and we ate it before, during, and after the main meal. I became, and remain, addicted to bread-dipping while drinking.

When I got hold of a copy of *Playboy's New Host and Bar Book* (1979), I scanned it for bread-dipping mixes and found none. The book had nothing on the subject. I checked to see who the author was—aha! Thomas Mario, an Italian. Italians have a rule about bread-dipping: don't do it! Why the prohibition on dipping? I'm not entirely sure, though several reasons have been suggested: (1) olive oil is too expensive, (2) Italians are aghast at the idea of communal dipping, (3) it spoils your appetite, (4) it makes you fat, (5) Italians don't like messy tables.

The Italians do have *fettunta*, from *fetta*, meaning "slice," and *unta*, meaning "oily." To celebrate the season's first olive oil, they make *fettunta* by grilling bread, rubbing it with a garlic clove, drizzling on olive oil, and sprinkling with sea salt. Chances are, however, that the visitor will not find *fettunta* in the restaurants, as it's not considered to be of restaurant quality.

We may disagree with Thomas Mario regarding bread-dipping, but we wholly concur with him when he says that "one of the best things about drinking is eating. Liquor allows people to unwind; hors d'oeuvres *and* liquor make them soar." The accurate translation of *hors d'oeuvres* is "apart from the work," but most of us translate it as "bite-sized." The food for drinking should be bite-sized, and, apart from encouraging bread-dipping, I will leave you with my favorite bite-sized shrimp recipe—one you will not find in the books.

We got this recipe from Mary Conroy, the wife of a colleague, some fifty years ago and use it often. If you try it with all due care, you may consider it worth the price of the book. The recipe calls for two pounds of shrimp, medium or large, headless, peeled, tails off.

Purchase fresh shrimp if you can manage it. It's been my experience that pre-cooked shrimp are always over-done and tougher than shrimp should be.

### Marinated Shrimp
2 pounds medium or large shrimp, heads and tails removed, peeled
2 large sweet onions, peeled
1 1/4 cups vegetable oil
3/4 cup white distilled (or any other light-colored) vinegar
1 1/2 teaspoons salt
2 1/2 teaspoons celery seed
A small jar of capers and their brine
A dash of Tabasco sauce

In a bowl, mix together the salt, celery seed, capers, and Tabasco until thoroughly combined. Set aside.

Bring a large pot of water to boil and add 1 pound (half) of the shrimp, letting them boil for no more than 2 minutes. Remove and allow them to cool while you cook the other pound of shrimp. Cut the onions into rings and separate them. Now put the shrimp, onions, oil, vinegar, and seasonings into a widemouthed jar or a one-gallon ziplock bag. Make certain the seal is tight because you must turn the container over a few times during its 24 hours (no less) of refrigeration.

To serve, remove the onions and the shrimp from the container and place them on a platter. If you're anything like me, you will like the onions as much as the shrimp.

# 14

## *Mixed Drinks for Every Occasion*

Very shortly after Prohibition became the law of the land, a malady of epidemic proportions spread across the nation. It was caused by the availability of moonshine and bathtub gin, and though it was never given a proper name, the journalist Amy Hopkins's term "burning palates" is certainly apt. The cure was to add taming ingredients to those beverages, thus making them drinkable. Milk, egg whites, lime juice, lemon juice, pomegranate, soda, mint, sugar, honey, grenadine syrup, and cherries were pressed into service, and "mixed drinks" largely replaced the earlier habit of "drinking it straight." Cocktails were invented in great numbers, some failing but many catching on as an improved way of taking alcohol.

Many people thought that as Prohibition passed away, so would the nation's newly acquired fondness for cocktails. The Irish journalist Maurice Gorham reported that cocktails "are not popular in London and when sold at all they are frequently poured from a bottle, which is all that people who want cocktails really deserve." The writer and diplomat Sir Leslie Shane (first cousin of Winston Churchill) insisted that cocktails "have all the disagreeability without the utility of a disinfectant."

What these he-men among imbibers choose to ignore is the fact that millions of us can't, won't, or prefer not to drink booze as it comes from the bottle, often harsh and too high in alcoholic content. On TV shows, one often notices that at day's end, the hero enjoys some kind of whiskey—about an inch of it, in a doubles glass. Ugh! It's warm and strong, and no doubt many like the jolt they get from it, but most of us don't, and if that were the only way to enjoy alcoholic beverages, we'd pass. It is solely because of cocktails and highballs that the joy of tippling exists for us. Here's to mixed drinks and to our heroes, both male and female, who invented them.

## The Mythical Martini

A myth, as the pundits tell us, is a "vital lie." Vital because it is necessary that someone believe it, and a lie because it isn't the truth. Most of the "Martinis" consumed today are not Martinis. What is served as a Martini and consumed as such is simply raw, cold gin in which an olive is briefly marinated. For it to qualify as a Martini, there must, of course, be vermouth in some proportion to the gin. Also, for the imbiber to qualify as a person of taste and discernment, there must be vermouth. But there ain't!

How do I know that the vermouth is missing? I'll get to that, but first let us briefly review the history of this most interesting drink, which is, after all, the premier world-class cocktail. There is no more touted and glorified drink on the planet. The writer and historian Bernard De Voto hailed it as "the supreme American gift to world culture." H. L. Mencken proclaimed it to be the only American invention "as perfect as a sonnet."

As of this writing, the Martini is probably 130 years old. In a wonderful book entitled *The Silver Bullet* (1981) and devoted entirely to the Martini, its author, Lowell Edmunds, contends that the first true Martini recipe was published in 1884. And me-oh-my did that original have vermouth! It was half gin, half vermouth, and that ratio is confirmed in *Grossman's Guide to Wines, Beers, and Spirits* (1983), where it is referred to as the "Traditional Martini."

As the reader well knows, tradition went out the window, way out! Not long after that first experiment came its more popular alternative, the "Dry Martini," which contained twice as much gin as vermouth. After that came the "Very Dry Martini" at a ratio of four to one. Harold Grossman recalled that the two-to-one "dry" was the more popular concoction before Prohibition, and that the four-to-one took its place somewhere between repeal and World War II.

The *Old Mr. Boston Deluxe Official Bartender's Guide* generally confirms this assessment. In my 1941 edition, a two-to-one is a "Dry Martini," but by the 1974 edition, that had become the "Traditional Martini" and the five-to-one became the "Dry Martini," and that holds through the 1988 edition.

As the country headed toward pure gin, however, the bar guides increasingly disagreed on the "true" proportions of this sacred tipple. Grossman gave in to the joke about the "Montgomery Martini" and reported the post–World War II Martini consisted of one part vermouth and fifteen parts gin (it was said that British General Montgomery would not go into battle unless his troops outnumbered the enemy's by at least fifteen to one). The *International Bartender's Guide*, by 1984, reported that the "Standard Dry Martini" consists of a ten-to-one mix. *Old Mr. Boston,* reflecting the respectability of its name, reported the "Extra Dry Martini" as having only eight parts of gin per one of vermouth.

Well before the guides abandoned reasonable standards, however, the consuming public had shown their utter disdain for them. Across the land, Martini drinkers remained calm when bartenders reached for the bottle of vermouth, but shouted bloody murder if they tipped the bottle to pour. Also, many complained, "Don't put those damned vegetables in there."

Tastes had outdistanced propriety. Americans craved gin straight and cold, but gin had a different pedigree from such potables as tequila and vodka, which may be taken "neat." It was not, and still is not, acceptable to take gin straight.

Tensions between peoples' desires and the constraints put upon them usually give rise to humor, and that has clearly been the case with the Martini. The humor, almost all of it, came to focus on how to add vermouth to the Martini without adding vermouth to the Martini. Again, I'll refer to Lowell Edmunds's book, which has a gold mine of the dodges. Seems that a man named Pool invented what he called "Martini Stones," which were actually marbles "soaked" in vermouth that could be added to the gin (one, I'm sure, would do the trick). Another fellow, Stanleigh by name, couched his dodge in the language of science:

A 60-watt incandescent lamp is placed on a flat surface 9 inches from a sealed bottle of vermouth. A sealed bottle of gin is placed on the other side of the bottle of vermouth at a distance of 23 inches. The lamp may be illuminated for an interval of 7 to 16 seconds.
The duration of exposure is governed by the color of the bottles.

My most recent brush with one of these myth-makers occurred at a function where I was introduced to a Martini man who, as our discussion proceeded, confided that he had achieved the "perfect Martini" without any fakery. With pride and enthusiasm he explained that all he had to do was put a bottle of suitable gin in his freezing compartment for one hour; then remove it and add to it vermouth in the ratio of one part vermouth to twenty parts gin, then return it to the freezing compartment for another ten minutes, and voilà! The perfect Martini.

"What about the *International Guide*'s contention that beyond the proportion of one part vermouth to ten parts gin, one simply cannot taste the vermouth?" I asked. The pitying wilt to his countenance more than suggested that anyone with even a modest meas-ure of breeding and discernment could and would taste the vermouth. Subsequently I looked further into the extent of the Martini's "dryness," in case I might be wrong in taking the *International Guide* as gospel. Sure enough, in consulting novelist Kingsley Amis (*On Drink* [1973]), I found that his recipe for a dry one has twelve to fifteen parts gin to one of vermouth.

I claimed early on that most Martinis have no vermouth in them at all. How would I know? I did the unforgiveable: I talked to the people who make them and to their managers and employers. What most bartenders discover is that no matter how much vermouth they add—rather, no matter how *little* vermouth they add—they get complaints. Nobody likes to take crap off a drunk, bartenders least of all. Most of them opt for the obvious solution and put it to the test. They make their "Martinis" with no vermouth, and, guess what, they get no complaints.

Personally, I find all of this delightfully entertaining in part because I am immune from any such deception. I don't like gin, and the Manhattan made with rye whiskey is my preference. But I realize that Martini fans harbor a passion and a loyalty that my kind can't match. Bernard De Voto exemplified that loyalty to the drink when he proclaimed that even one's demeanor should be proper when making them.

The goal is purification and that will begin after the first round has been poured, so I see no need for preliminary spiritual exercises.

But it is best approached with a tranquil mind, lest the necessary speed become haste. Tranquility ought normally to come with the sight of the familiar bottles. If it doesn't, feel free to hum some simple tune as you go about your preparations; it should be nostalgic but not sentimental, neither barbershop nor jazz, between the choir and the glee club. Do not whistle, for your companions are sinking into the quiet of expectation. And you need not sing, for presently there will be singing in your heart.

De Voto insisted that only two cocktails were worthy of consideration: the Martini and a slug of whiskey. To make the latter, he wrote, you pour some whiskey on some ice. His version of the Martini had a four-to-one mix using Plymouth Gin and Dolin dry vermouth. Both beverages were to be as cold as possible, short of freezing. In front of me is a book by Sally Ann Berk entitled *The Martini Book* (2007) that contains 201 recipes, all of which are versions of, or related to, the Martini. Among the 201, I counted 137 called Martinis, but among them there is no mention of the most popular version of all: straight gin.

## 𝓕our 𝓜ixed 𝓓rinks

I am devoted, really devoted, to four mixed drinks, and I hope my experience with them will encourage a few kindred spirits among you.

### Manhattan

The first, and most special, of mixed drinks is the Manhattan, now the king of cocktails (after the downfall of the Martini). Perfecting the Manhattan is no easy task, but I know many readers will doubt what I say because it contains no more than whiskey, sweet vermouth, and a dash or two of bitters (and for some, a cherry); what's so difficult about that? In his delightful, *Boozehound: On the Trail of the Rare, the Obscure, and the Overrated in Spirits* (2010), journalist Jason Wilson explains it well:

> The Manhattan is more complex than the Martini and more flavorful. Like a strong poetic structure, the Manhattan recipe is more of a starting point than a rote list of ingredients. It is both universal and highly personal. The Manhattan encourages modifications, rifts, virtuoso performances.

> The typical bar guide's recipe will produce a good drink unless cheap ingredients are used or the bartender forgets the bitters, but why settle for good when *wondrous* can be achieved? What the reader should

realize is that this drink, carefully concocted, can be as the writer and cocktail historian David Wondrich put it, "relaxing as a deep massage."

The first decision, and many would agree the most important, is which whiskey to use. In the years before Prohibition, rye whiskey was heavily favored, but afterward bourbon took over. There is a substantial difference. Rye is the stronger of the two, not necessarily in ABV but in its ability to hold its flavor against the vermouth. By comparison with rye, bourbon and sweet vermouth yield a mixture that is "sticky sweet," as Wondrich put it. One might go so far as to say that if you want an aperitif, use rye, but if you want an after-dinner drink, use bourbon.

Eighty-five years after Prohibition ended, rye's popularity is on the rise; it is now the "comeback kid" among spirits, and no drink has had more to do with its return than the Manhattan. The continuing use of bourbon in the United States today is strongest down where "bourbon" is pronounced without the *r* sound. Blended whiskey is also recommended in several guides, and then there is this from the renowned David Embury in his book *The Fine Art of Mixing Drinks* (1958). After recounting the usual Manhattan recipes, he writes:

The above Manhattan recipes are given for general information only. Once again, I recommend that you forget them all and that in your own home you serve the following:

### Manhattan Deluxe
1 part Cinzano Italian Vermouth
5 parts Bonded Whiskey
1 dash Angostura to each drink

Here, "bonded" whiskey is important because, at 100 proof (50 percent ABV as opposed to the usual 40 percent) you have the strongest whiskey with the least vermouth of any Manhattan recipe you'll find.

If you have any faith in taste tests, in 2014, *Huffington Post* put twenty-four rye–Italian vermouth combinations up for comparison with interesting results. The ryes varied in price from $18 to $66, and the question to be answered was, Does expensive rye and vermouth improve the Manhattan? Conclusion: no! The top three combinations were as follows:

Best in Show: Wild Turkey rye ($23) with Maurin vermouth ($22)

Highly Recommended: Rittenhouse rye ($26) with Martini vermouth ($11)

Highly Recommended: Old Overholt rye ($18) with Vya vermouth ($22)

All the drinks in this taste test were made in the ratio of two parts rye whiskey to one part vermouth, and to each drink a few drops of Angostura bitters were added. The drinks were stirred, not shaken. The panel of taste experts was not described. A graph of the results was presented, and the line of "best fit" between taste and price showed a slight downward slant.

As for red or sweet vermouths, there's a lot of them and a lot of difference between them. The highest praise (and a high price) usually goes to Carpano Antica. Martini Rosso is sweet both in taste and price, and Vya is for you if you like a spicier drink. Dolin and Cocchi also get frequent mention. Here's to hoping your store has a wide selection. Mine doesn't. Never forget the bitters, and for a Manhattan they should be the aromatic kind; Angostura is by far the most popular, and rightly so.

In his *The Stork Club Bar Book* (1946), newspaper columnist Lucius Beebe makes an interesting comment: "It has often been remarked that the most exciting Manhattan is one compounded with ordinary quality bar whisky rather than the rarest overproof article." I suspect it may be a matter of whether the bartender adds bitters or fails to do so. A serious criticism of the Manhattan comes from Kingsley Amis in his *On Drink*, where he contends that it's what you drink if you're too lazy to build an Old-Fashioned.

145

After giving the recipe for a Manhattan he writes: "Whatever the pundits may say, this is in practice the not very energetic man's Old-Fashioned, and is an excellent drink, though never, I think, as good as a properly made Old-Fashioned."

## Old-Fashioned

Ever have your cage rattled? That comment did it for me. I'd been experimenting with Manhattans for years with nary a thought to the Old-Fashioned. I immediately got hold of David Embury's *The Fine Art of Mixing Drinks* and read everything he had to say about the drink. The first thing I learned was that Kingsley Amis didn't know how to make sugar syrup, or simple syrup as some call it, and that's why he considered making an Old-Fashioned "work." If you don't have the syrup, you must put a sugar cube in the bottom of the glass and add just enough lukewarm water to cover it completely. When it starts to dissolve, you must crush it with a muddler and then mix it with one to three dashes of Angostura bitters. If you have the syrup, just add a teaspoon or two and stir it with the bitters. Then you add a jigger of rye, bourbon, or brandy, the ice, and a lemon rind if you wish.

According to Embury, it takes about twenty minutes to make an Old-Fashioned if you don't have the syrup, and about two minutes if you do. He also insists that the syrup makes a better drink. I made the syrup according to his instructions, and it's very easy. Put a saucepan on the stove and add three cups of sugar to it; then add one cup of water and stir until the sugar is dissolved. Boil the mixture for a few minutes, then let it cool and bottle it. He used old pint liquor bottles with screw tops; I used empty Zero Coke bottles.

Embury found that most people like one teaspoonful of sugar and one to two dashes of Angostura to two ounces of whiskey. He absolutely insists that the Old-Fashioned contain no water lest the drink become a short highball instead of a cocktail. Some recipes do call for water.

Is the Old-Fashioned superior to the Manhattan? If you have a sweet tooth it may well be. I certainly would say that if you have a bottle of whiskey that isn't first rate, the Old-Fashioned would be a good way of getting rid of it. In any case, if you keep a bar in your home and don't have that supply of sugar syrup, it might be well worth your while to add it.

### Rusty Nail

My third cocktail puts no mixing burden on you at all, since it is, as David Wondrich observed, a drink of "foolproof construction." You can't screw this one up! The Rusty Nail is no more than a mixture of good Scotch and Drambuie, the famous liqueur that derives from it. Recipe ratios vary from half-and-half to four-to-one, and they're all good. Your choice will probably depend on the extent to which Scotch is your friend. If the drink is too sweet, add more Scotch, and if it's too dry, add more Drambuie. As both the Scotch and the Drambuie are 80 proof, this is a strong drink.

Invented in 1937 and credited to one F. Benniman, the Rusty Nail was first named the B.I.F. (British Industries Fair); in the United States it became the D&S. The bartenders at New York's fashionable Club 21 offered it as the Rusty Nail. When the swank Little Club on East 55th Street took it on, it became "Little Club No. 1," and in the upper Midwest it was called a Knucklehead. Then, in 1963, Gina MacKinnon, chairwoman of the Drambuie Liqueur Company endorsed "Rusty Nail" in the *New York Times*, and that settled the matter. It has been suggested that the name came from Scottish bartenders who repaid noisy American customers by mixing their drinks with a rusty nail. Another part of the lore has it that the drink was favored by the members of the Rat Pack, and that contributed to the drink's popularity. The Rusty Nail has also gained the reputation of being the favorite drink of "depressed old men."

The Scotches most often recommended for the Rusty Nail are the better blends. Often listed are the following: Dewars 12, Johnny Walker Black, The

Famous Grouse, J&B, and Chivas Regal. David Wondrich also suggests that the low-cost single malt Bowmore Legend makes a good Rusty Nail. The lemon garnish, the stemmed cherry, and bitters all seem optional with this drink. Most take it over ice.

## Smith and Kearns

After three whiskey drinks, my fourth and final is a departure. It is meek and mild to be sure, but it is very popular in my house. Thanks to Eric Felten (*Wall Street Journal*, 23 September 2006), we know the exact origin of this drink. During the North Dakota oil boom of the 1950s, two oil men named Wendell Smith and James Currans stayed at the Prince Hotel in Bismarck and would end their days down in the Blue Blazer Lounge. One day, after a very liquid evening in the lounge, the two men asked bartender "Shorty" Doebber if he could make something to improve their condition. Shorty came up with a following drink, which he built in a tall glass by combining 2 ounces crème de cacao, 1/2 ounce club soda, and 1 ounce half-and-half with several ice cubes. He stirred it briefly so as not to lose the fizz from the club soda. The drink was originally dubbed the "Smith and Currans," and it caught on quickly among the regulars; as oil men travel a lot, word of mouth spread widely before the correct spelling made it into the bar guides. In my guides, there is a "Smith and Kerns" and "Smith and Kearns"—the latter won out and that's what I call it here.

This cacao-flavored (chocolate) drink need not be carefully measured. Further, one can substitute Kahlúa at 40 percent ABV for the stronger crème de cacao's 50 percent. I serve it often, and make my own coffee liqueur as follows: Put a large pot on the stove. Add 8 cups of sugar and 8 cups of water. Stir well and low boil for an hour. Turn off the burner and add 8 cups of the cheapest vodka you can find. Add 1 1/2 cups of instant coffee and 2 tablespoons of vanilla. Bottle when cool. I've made Smith and Kearns without the soda, having run out—it's not as good that way.

In 1991, I attended a conference that ended with a fine dinner at which I was seated with five women at a table for six. We had fun as everybody joined in lively conversation, and I felt compelled to treat my new friends to an after-dinner drink. I walked to the bar and asked the bartender if he knew how to make a Smith and Kearns. Indeed he did, and the ladies downed $85 worth of them. Not all that impressive today, but that was a quarter of a century ago!

The Smith and Kearns is a light drink well-suited for those who will drive home, and for those who simply don't want very much to drink. Also sometimes when "the gang's all here," and we're having such a good time, I get that terrible feeling that I've had a bit too much to drink. Then I make a Smith and Kearns, sip a little, and sit back and let metabolism work its magic. For all to see, I'm still "drinking with the crowd," but, in fact, I'm taking the cure.

These four drinks are all I make on a regular basis, never having liked rum, gin, or vodka. I may dabble on the holidays but not seriously. I make the Smith and Kearns at the drop of a hat for my guests, but only the strong stuff on request.

Again, those who eschew mixed drinks puzzle me greatly. I won't say that they are too lazy to extend the little bit of effort involved in making them. I won't say that following recipes is too much for them. I won't say that they are just in a hurry to get high. I won't say anything derogatory about them. But I will say that they are missing some of the greatest-tasting stuff made by man.

## Not Found in the Bar Guides

Boredom being pandemic in these United States, I offer the following drinks that some of you may wish to try for want of anything better to do.

### Say Sour

Here is a drink that doesn't make it into the books but should. I got this simple recipe from a Canadian bartender working for a while in the United States. He called this drink "Say Sour" and made it by simply substituting a bit of Amaretto for the sugar in an ordinary Whiskey Sour recipe. It should not be confused with the usual Amaretto Sour, which I find far too sweet. Unfortunately, I didn't find out how much Amaretto to add, but it should lend to a little experimenting.

## Hot Brick

Here is a toddy that allows a rare opportunity to compare modern-day taste to the "good old days." The original recipe, near as I can determine, was as follows.

### Original Hot Brick
1 cup sugar
1 cup butter
2 cups bourbon whiskey

Combine the ingredients in a small pan, bring to a boil, and serve.

What follows is the modern and highly modified version consistently given through several editions of *Old Mr. Boston*'s guide.

### Modern Hot Brick
1 teaspoon butter
1 teaspoon powdered sugar

3 pinches cinnamon
1 ounce hot water

Dissolve the above thoroughly, then add 1 1/2 ounces bourbon or rye whiskey. Fill the glass with boiling water and stir.

The earlier version was intended for hunters who hit a hard trail after rising early on a frosty morning. The latter, apparently, is more suited to the white-collar dude who faces nothing more brisk than the walk to his car.

## The Hunter's Flask

The mention of hunters brings to mind the question of what went into those little flasks that they carried into the field with them. We know them now as "hip flasks," but to my mind they should be "nip flasks," as they are of such diminished capacity that a generous swallow would all but empty them. Early on, hunter's flasks were larger, holding eight or ten ounces in heavy borosilicate glass within thick leather cases and holding enough to share with others. But what typically goes into those flasks? I had thought Scotch, bourbon, rye, or gin, but that notion overlooked the thought and care that went into having the best drink in the hunting party.

Gin with a dozen cloves was popular, as is sloe gin with vanilla. Probably most common today is the habit of putting one's favorite cocktail in the flask. Thanks to publisher John Van Voorst, who in 1869 came out with *Cups and Their Customs*, however, we have the recipe that poet Robert Burns used to fill his hunting flask.

### The Robert Burns

To a quart of whiskey add the rinds of two lemons, an ounce of bruised ginger, and a pound of white ripe currants stripped from their stalks. Put these ingredients into a covered vessel and let them stand for a few days; then strain carefully, and add one pound of powdered loaf sugar. This may be bottled two days after the sugar has been added.

## Bullshot

John Doxat, author of *The World of Drinks and Drinking* (1971) is keen on Bullshot, which may be viewed as an alternative to the Bloody Mary. Doxat calls it a "splendid restorative." I pass along his version because it differs from bar guide versions, and because of his enthusiasm for this "morning after" consoler. You may wish to introduce it in the morning after you and your loved one both overindulged a bit, since the recipe is for two people.

### Bullshot for Two
1 can Campbell's condensed consommé
2 ounces Cossack Vodka

1 teaspoon Worcestershire sauce
Dash each of cayenne, celery salt, and Tabasco
sauce

Mix all ingredients vigorously with lots of ice and strain
into tumblers. Note: The use of tumblers suggests a
home version. In bars, such drinks are served in large,
chilled wine glasses in the manner of Bloody Marys.

## Two Liqueurs

If you want Baileys, you can find a recipe for it on the
internet. This one, from my wife's cousin Jeannie Ni-
sius, is a bit simpler and mighty fine.

### Jeanne's Irish Cream
1 1/2 cups Canadian whiskey
1 pint whipping cream
2 eggs
1 can condensed milk (not evaporated)
2 to 4 tablespoons chocolate syrup
1 tablespoon vanilla or almond flavoring

In a blender, combine all the ingredients. Blend and
serve. Any amount left over must be kept refrigerated
and shaken before using.

The second concoction is a cherry liqueur, which
I include because it saves all the work of preparing

actual cherries. The simplicity of this one may cause you to doubt its value; I can only encourage you to give it a try if you like cherry flavor.

**Cherry Cordial**
1 fifth of tawny port
1 cup sugar
1 pint cherry brandy

Pour the tawny port into a saucepan and simmer for half an hour. Let it cool for 2 hours. Add the sugar and the brandy, stir, and bottle.

## Postgate's Aperitif Wines

If you wish to dabble with aperitif wines, one place to start is with two versions created by John Postgate and his father (the latter was a wine expert of some renown). Both men found that their wives didn't care for their productions, which may mean that they take a little getting used to.

The one they labeled "Solace" is certainly easy. To one bottle of cheap white port, add a thimble of Campari and the zest of 2 square centimeters of an orange. Do not use essence of orange, they warned, or the results will be "really nasty." Also, that amount of zest seems to be critical.

Their other version, "Postgate's Corsican Aperitif," calls for British ruby or tawny wine of "port character"—the cheaper the better, as is also suggested for the above. Add 2 to 4 drops of quinine bitters and 2 or 3 drops of vanilla essence. Cork and set aside for three weeks. They kept some for six months with no appreciable improvement in taste. But, they insist, it does take three weeks at room temperature to transform a "vanilla-flavored port into a drink with its own character."

## Tom and Jerry Tip

Tom and Jerrys have made many of my Christmas times merry, and this trick makes them much easier to concoct. The normal recipe, you may know, involves a batter that lasts a third of a day at best. It is made by separating the whites from the yolks, beating each separately, then folding them together with sugar, rum, Angostura bitters, vanilla extract, and spices. If one uses only the egg whites, however, the batter can be frozen and used over and over again. The drink is made by putting the batter in a Tom and Jerry cup, or small mug, adding rum and Cognac, and filling to the brim with steaming milk. A little grated nutmeg is a nice touch.

**Easy Gin Punch**

I found this one by returning again to *Cups and Their Customs*:

> Stir the rind of a lemon and half its juice, in a half-pint of gin; add a glass of Maraschino, half a pint of water and two tablespoons of pounded white sugar, and, immediately before serving, pour in two bottles of iced soda water.

# The Nightcap

The etymologists tell us that the word *nightcap* took on a second meaning in 1818, when it could refer either to the cap worn to bed, as it always had, or to the last drink of the day. The latter meaning, since the introduction of central heating, has taken over, and many people today are not aware that a cap might well have been worn to bed on chilly nights.

Before it was discovered that an alcoholic nightcap doesn't make for the best night's rest, it was prescribed by doctors for those having trouble getting to sleep. Now that sleep is better understood, modern medicine advises against the nightcap. We are told that there are two kinds of sleep, deep sleep or SWS (slow-wave sleep) and REM (rapid eye movement) sleep. Normally, your first phase is REM sleep, the "dream sleep" stage that lasts about an hour and a half. Then you fall into deep sleep, during which the body restores itself. Most of a night's sleep is SWS, but the two types alternate.

Although a nightcap will get you to sleep faster, it will be deep sleep, robbing you of the initial REM or "dream sleep." Further, people who drink nightcaps find that the second half of their seven or eight hours in bed will be fitful compared to the first half. It is also contended that the sleep-inducing benefits of nightcaps don't last as the body adapts to alcohol's effects.

The message in all of this is not to drink nightcaps on a regular basis. The seasoned tippler knows when to indulge, knows when to end the day in that blissful little indulgence that warms the throat and soothes the soul. But what shall it be? Let us first turn to Rosie Schaap who writes the "Drink" column for the *New York Times Magazine*. She offers four rules for achieving the "honorable" nightcap: (1) one drink only, (2) the liquor should be brown—no gin or vodka allowed, (3) the drink should be warming, and (4) the drink shouldn't stray far from what you've had earlier in the evening. If you've been drinking wine, she suggests Cognac; if blended whiskey, a single malt scotch. Ms. Schaap's "honorable" nightcaps pretty well describe the current preferences.

David Wondrich, on the other hand, tells us of three mixed drinks that have served well as nightcaps:

The Stinger, which combines 2 1/4 ounces of Cognac with 3/4 ounce of white crème de menthe; the Kneecap, made with 1 1/2 ounces of bourbon and 1 1/2 ounces of ruby port; and the Velour, consisting of 2 1/4 ounces of white crème de menthe and 3/4 ounce of crème de cassis. All three are to be shaken with lots of ice, then strained into a chilled cocktail glass. As all three require ice and chilled glasses, they run afoul of Ms. Schaap's rule calling for warmth in the nightcap. This is par for the course, as it would be hard to find a subject on which there is less agreement than on the question of what constitutes the ideal nightcap.

Even beer is preferred by many as the ideal nightcap. In Danish, for example, there is the word *godnatbajer*, which translates as "goodnight beer." In Belgium, there is the Slaapmutske brewery, and *slaapmutske* in English is "nightcap." In Northern Ireland, there is the Night Cap Beer Company. In the United States, cocktails dominate the nightcap realm, but in Europe it would seem to be beer, save for Scotland, of course.

Here in the United States, we have at least three recipes named either "Nightcap" or "Night Cap." Here they are:

**Nightcap No. 1**
6 ounces milk
1 teaspoon powdered sugar

1 ounce Kahlúa
Dash of nutmeg

Heat the milk, add the sugar and Kahlúa. Sprinkle nutmeg on top and serve.

### Night Cap No. 2
1 ounce anisette liqueur
1 ounce curaçao liqueur
1 ounce brandy
Yolk of 1 egg

Combine the ingredients, shake well with ice, and strain into a glass.

### Night Cap No. 3
2 ounces rum
1 teaspoon powdered sugar

Combine the rum and sugar in a Tom and Jerry mug and add enough warm milk to fill it. Grate a little nutmeg on top.

Oftentimes, the nightcap is counted on to relieve an overstuffed stomach. Speaking to that need, the journalist Brent Rose suggests several digestifs, or aids to digestion. His first suggestion is bitters, such as Angostura, taken by the teaspoonful or dissolved in sparkling water, a nonalcoholic drink some call a "mocktail." More to our taste are liqueurs such as that wonderful creation of the Carthusian monks, Chartreuse; or the Italian Campari; or Fernet, which seems on its way to becoming the national drink of Argentina. He also recognizes the value of mint to the ailing tummy and suggests two ounces of brandy added to a six-ounce cup of peppermint tea.

Wine is gaining popularity as a nightcap, particularly among women who have replaced evening snacks with a glass or two. A Harvard study of twenty-thousand female wine drinkers discovered, after thirteen years, that 70 percent of them were less likely to be overweight. Red wine is the more effective in this regard, in part because it can help transform stubborn white fat into burnable brown fat.

The preference for brown spirits in our nightcaps has kept gin and vodka out of the running, but with the popularity of vodka in the United States, inroads are inevitable. The first we've found is "Lavender Honey Cream." In this recipe, the word *vodka* does not appear. It is represented as "Square One Botanical Spirit."

My nightcap is the good old Rusty Nail (see page 103). In all the literature I've read on nightcaps, it gets no mention. Checking the internet, however, I found one writer who suggested that it *can* serve as a nightcap, though it is a bit strong. But what's life without a few risks?

# 15

## *Final Tips for Tipplers*

In America, the land where people mind one another's business to a fault, tipplers should be reminded that matters relating to alcohol are taken more seriously than in the Western world as a whole. Therefore, at the risk of insult, I take it upon myself to remind dear readers of the inviolate with a few exhortations.

> "Never allow children to mix drinks. It is unseemly and they use too much vermouth." (Fran Lebowitz)
>
> "Never lie in a bar. You may, however, grossly exaggerate." (Anonymous)

"Never measure masculinity with a shot glass."
(Jimmy the Bartender)

"Never cry over spilt milk. It could have been whiskey." (Pappy Maverick)

"Never, never trust anyone who asks for white wine. It means they're phonies." (Bette Davis)

"Never worry about being driven to drink; just worry about being driven home." (W. C. Fields)

"Never wear sunglasses to a cocktail party." (Anonymous)

"Never follow whiskey with port." (P. V. Taylor)

"Never drink and drive—you might spill some." (Tom Egan)

# Afterword

Years ago, at the behest of the University of West Florida's provost, I undertook an examination of Ray Oldenburg's academic credentials, including a careful reading of his major work, *The Great Good Place: Cafés, Coffee Shops, Community Centers, Beauty Parlors, General Stores, Bars, Hangouts, and How They Get you Through the Day*. His accomplishments, especially with the publication of that book, were impressive. In December 1996, I joined his department as a visiting professor of sociology. He and I became friends and, over the course of more than twenty years, good friends.

I raise the matter of friendship because I believe that friendship is what prompted an invitation to pen a brief afterword for his latest book, *The Joy of Tippling*. How else could one explain the irony involved in selecting a teetotaler to close out a volume on drinking crafted by the ultimate tippler? There is an outside chance that another factor may have played a small role in that selection: I do actually partake of one, and only one, libation per year, and that drink is typically mixed by Professor Oldenburg and consumed in his Pensacola "man cave"—his own little great good place.

Nevertheless, a sober reading of *The Joy of Tippling* is all I am capable of, and that sober reading finds the book packed with factual information, humor and wit, personal insights, and sound sociological observations. Here the primary focus will be on the last of these features, and especially on Oldenburg's observations of and insights into the social solidarity-generating and community-saving (and perhaps community-building) nature of tippling.

One does not have to read too far in *The Joy of Tippling* before the author's image of humans emerges. He sees us as profoundly social animals. We are by nature cooperative, more than competitive, critters; our progress through time has depended on that cooperation. It is our species-specific characteristic. We consciously and cooperatively produce life's necessities. And anything and everything that imperils such cooperation needs to be mightily combatted.

We cooperate in social settings, and as Oldenburg points out, these are actual physical entities—a point either missed or purposely ignored by too many sociologists. Such places are the prime focus of his best-known book, and they play a prominent role and are nicely dealt with in *The Joy of Tippling.* To destroy the places where tipplers gather is to lessen social solidarity, weaken our sense of community, and maybe even, believe it or not, strike a blow at our essential humanity.

As a representative of an old-fashioned intellectual tradition in sociology, I believe that people in concert can and should modify, rework, and/or take down those repressive social arrangements that confront them and whose harmful consequences they must suffer. Such radical resistance and reconstruction become more difficult as a host of forces (e.g., suburban sprawl, freeway construction, renewal/removal projects, and white flight) combine, whether consciously or not, with puritans, meddlers, moral crusaders, religious fundamentalists, and politicians to both cut down on the number of places where tipplers congregate, and to prevent the birth of others. Not an irrational action on their part: in vino veritas. Those whose tongues have been loosened by the moderate consumption of alcohol have been known to speak the unspeakable, to reveal the ugly truth that "all is not well with the kingdom." Close the place, eliminate the discourse, stifle another source of disruptive action. What could be more rational for those in power?

All this brings me to a criticism of *The Joy of Tippling*, one that applies equally to *The Great Good Place*: Places where folks congregate (whether to eat, drink, work on joint projects, or simply talk) may indeed promote solidarity on the part of those so gathered, as Oldenburg repeatedly demonstrates. But of equal or greater importance, they also provide forums for expressing discontent, for fomenting and then perhaps acting on those ideas that challenge the status quo. More attention needs to be paid to great good places in general, and drinking establishments in particular, as real sources of meaningful social change.

If we are to avoid what sociologist Michael Schwalbe has called "the seductions of false community" and begin the long march back to democracy and real community, we will have to start in the states, and within the states in the streets, but maybe also in those establishments frequented by moderate drinkers. There have been many drunken acts of riot and destruction, including a well-documented beer-hall putsch. But there have also been tavern rebellions. Tipplers to the barricades!

In closing, I note that *The Joy of Tippling* highlights several good reasons for being a moderate drinker, and several more for neither abstaining nor overindulging. If you are not already familiar with them or if you wish to have at your disposal additional facts to aid in defending tippling to hostile others, by all means read this book.

Kindly pass it on to associates and encourage still others to read it; then everyone get together over drinks at your favorite place. Such behavior promotes solidarity, shores up a sense of community, and may well encourage the type of radical action required if ours is to become a more reasonable, decent, just, civil, and free society. We need such action nowadays, as the widely respected publication *The Economist*, in its annual Democracy Index, has downgraded the United States of America from a "full democracy" to a "flawed democracy."

Lastly, we know that heavy drinkers are seldom destined for great longevity, but Professor Oldenburg has a warning for the teetotalers. It is summed up in an old Kingston Trio hit:

Here's to the man who drinks water pure and goes
    to bed quite sober.
He falls as the leaves do fall,
He falls as the leaves do fall,
He falls as the leaves do fall,
He'll die before October.

For the tippler, Oldenburg is the bearer of happy tidings, also conveyed by the Trio:

Here's to the man who drinks dark ale and goes to
    bed quite mellow!

He lives as he ought to live,
He lives as he ought to live,
He lives as he ought to live,
He'll die a jolly good fellow.

Apparently, tipplers live longer. I certainly hope Ray Oldenburg does! Many of us have derived considerable pleasure from reading his published work. *The Joy of Tippling* also pleases. It is indeed a good read.

Larry T. REYNOLDS
Central Michigan University

# Books for Tipplers

Amis, Kingsley. *On Drink*. New York: Harcourt Brace Jovanovich, 1973.

Barr, Andrew. *Drink: A Social History of America*. New York: Carroll & Graf, 1999.

Beebe, Lucius. *The Stork Club Bar Book*. New York: Rinehart & Company, 1946.

Berk, Sally Ann. *The Martini Book: 201 Ways to Mix the Perfect American Cocktail*. Rev. ed. New York: Black Dog & Leventhal, 2007.

Brown, Bob. *Let There Be Beer!* New York: H. Smith & R. Haas, 1932.

Chafetz, Morris E. *Liquor: The Servant of Man*. Boston: Little, Brown, 1965.

Doxat, John. *The World of Drinks and Drinking: An International Distillation*. New York: Drake Publishers, 1971.

Edgley, Charles and Dennis Brissett. *A Nation of Meddlers*. Boulder, CO: Westview Press, 2000.

Embury, David A. *The Fine Art of Mixing Drinks*. 2nd rev. ed. New York: Doubleday, 1958.

Federle, Tim. *Tequila Mockingbird: Cocktails with a Literary Twist*. Philadelphia: Running Press, 2013.

Ford, Gene. *The French Paradox & Drinking for Health*. San Francisco: Wine Appreciation Guild, 1993.

Grossman, Harold J. *Grossman's Guide to Wines, Beers, and Spirits*. New York: Macmillan, 1983.

Lees, Frederic Richard. *The Temperance Bible Commentary: Giving at One View, Version, Criticism, and Exposition, in Regard to All Passages of Holy Writ Bearing on 'Wine' and 'Strong Drink.'* New York: Sheldon & Co., 1870.

Mario, Thomas. *Playboy's New Host and Bar Book*. Chicago: Playboy Press, 1979.

Mooney, Sean. *Sean Mooney's Practical Guide to Running a Pub*. Chicago: Nelson-Hall, 1979.

*The New International Bartender's Guide*. New York: Random House, 1984.

*Old Mr. Boston Deluxe Official Bartender's Guide*. Boston: Mr. Boston Distiller Corporation, 1974.

Oldenburg, Ray, ed. *Celebrating the Third Place: Inspiring Stories about the "Great Good Places" at the Heart of Our Communities*. New York: Marlow & Company, 2001.

Oldenburg, Ray. *The Great Good Place: Cafés, Coffee Shops, Community Centers, Beauty Parlors, General Stores, Bars, Hangouts, and How They Get You Through the Day.* New York: Paragon House, 1989.

Powers, Madelon. *Faces Along the Bar: Lore and Order in the Workingman's Saloon, 1870–1920.* Chicago: University of Chicago Press, 1998.

Roberts, George Edwin. *Cups and Their Customs.* London: J. Van Voorst, 1863.

Rogers, Adam. *Proof: The Science of Booze.* New York: Houghton Mifflin Harcourt, 2014.

Schaap, Rosie. *Drinking with Men: A Memoir.* New York: Riverhead Books, 2013.

Schivelbusch, Wolfgang. *Tastes of Paradise: A Social History of Spices, Stimulants, and Intoxicants.* Translated by David Jacobson. New York: Pantheon Books, 1992. See esp. chap. 7, "Drinking Places."

Tebeau, John. *Bars, Taverns, and Dives New Yorkers Love.*

Wilson, Jason. *Boozehound: On the Trail of the Rare, the Obscure, and the Overrated in Spirits.* Berkeley, CA: Ten Speed Press, 2010.

Wondrich, David. *Imbibe! From Absinthe Cocktail to Whiskey Smash, a Salute in Stories and Drinks to "Professor" Jerry Thomas, Pioneer of the American Bar.* Updated and rev. ed. New York: Perigree, 2015.

# *Movies*

*The Angels' Share,* Ken Loach 2012

*Apocalypse Now,* Francis Coppola 1979

*Arthur,* Steve Gordon 1981, Oak Bar (Plaza)

*Barfly,* Barbet Schroeder, 1987

*Beerfest,* Jay Chandrasekhar 2006

*Bridesmaids ,* Paul Feig 2011, Norman One Step

*Casablanca,* Michael Curtiz 1942, Rick's Café Americain

*Cocktail,* Roger Donaldson 1988, Baker Street Pub

*Good Will Hunting,* Gus Van Sant 1997, L Street Tavern

*Goodfellas,* Martin Scorsese 1990, Neir's Tavern and Bamboo Lounge

*Identity Thief,* Seth Gordon 2013

*It's A Wonderful Life,* Frank Capra 1946, Martini's/ Nick's

*Leaving Las Vegas,* Mike Figgis 1995, Boardner's

*Mean Streets,* Martin Scorsese 1973, Via Tutto

*The Shining,* Stanley Kubrick 1980, The Gold Bar

*Shaun of the Dead,* Edgar Wright 2004, The Winchester

*Star Wars: A New Hope,* George Lucas 1977, Mos Eisley Cantina

*Trainspotting,* Danny Boyle 1996, Crosslands Pub

*Wedding Singer,* Frank Coraci, 1998, Avignone's

*Withnail & I*, Bruce Robinson 1987
*The World's End*, Edgar Wright 2013

## 𝒯𝑒𝑙𝑒𝑣𝑖𝑠𝑖𝑜𝑛𝑠 𝒮𝒽𝑜𝑤𝑠

*Arrested Development*, United States, Fox/Netflix, 2003–2006, 2013–present, C.W. Swappigan's

*Cheers*, United States, NBC, 1982–1993, Cheers

*How I Met Your Mother*, United States, CBS, 2005–2014, MacLaren's

*It's Always Sunny in Philadelphia*, United States, FX, 2005–2012, Paddy's

*Mad Men*, United States, AMC, 2007–2015, Grand Central Oyster Bar

*Only Fools and Horses*, United Kingdom, BBC, 1981–2003, Nags Head

*Parks and Recreation*, United States, NBC, 2009–2015, Paddy's Pub

*The Simpsons*, United States, Fox, 1989–present, Moe's

*The Sopranos*, United States, HBO, 1999–2007

*True Blood*, United States, HBO, 2008–2014, Alex's

# Index

Ray Oldenburg is known internationally for his book *The Great Good Place: Cafes, Coffee Shops, Bookstores, Bars, Hair Salons, and Other Hangouts at the Heart of a Community*, a surprise hit when it appeared in 1989. Starbucks even asked Oldenburg to endorse their coffee shops (he declined). He has advised cities including San Jose, Stockholm, and Osaka on community development, and often hosts friends in his own converted-garage saloon in Pensacola, Florida. His favorite drink is a Manhattan.